THE ULTIMATE
Big Green Egg®
Cookbook
AN INDEPENDENT GUIDE

100 MASTER RECIPES
for Perfect Smoking, Grilling and Baking

CHRIS SUSSMAN
Founding Member of BGE Team Green and
creator of The BBQ Buddha™

PAGE STREET
PUBLISHING CO.

PAGE STREET
PUBLISHING CO.

Copyright © 2023 Chris Sussman

First published in 2023 by
Page Street Publishing Co.
27 Congress Street, Suite 1511
Salem, MA 01970
www.pagestreetpublishing.com

Distributed by Macmillan, sales in Canada by The Canadian Manda Group.

The Big Green Egg, convEGGtor and EGGcessories are trademarks of The Big Green Egg, Inc., which did not sponsor, authorize or endorse this book.

27   26   25   24   23   2   3   4   5

ISBN-13: 978-1-64567-730-7
ISBN-10: 1-64567-730-3

Library of Congress Control Number: 2022945412

Cover and book design by Rosie Stewart for Page Street Publishing Co.
Photography by Chris Sussman

Printed and bound in the United States of America

Page Street Publishing protects our planet by donating to nonprofits like The Trustees, which focuses on local land conservation.

I dedicate this book to my family: Debbie, Jessica, Zachary, Yoda and Obi. All of you inspire me so much every day. I love you all.

CHAPTER 4

The convEGGtor Is the Way

Roasting, Baking and More

CHAPTER 5

Can You Really Do That?

Recipes to Harness All the Add-Ons the Big Green Egg Has to Offer

Introduction

So you bought a Big Green Egg®, and you have no idea where to start. Or maybe you have done a few cooks on your Big Green Egg but need some inspiration. Perhaps you bought your Big Green Egg for grilling, and you want to learn how to harness all the abilities this cooker has to offer. Or you are a seasoned EGGhead looking to expand your culinary adventures on this amazing grill. No matter where you are on this spectrum, this book is for you.

My name is Chris Sussman, a.k.a. The BBQ Buddha™. I am a member of the Big Green Egg Pro Staff and author of the book *The Four Fundamentals of Smoking*. I have been cooking on a Big Green Egg since 2009 and have hosted countless classes around the country, teaching people how to master this amazing grill. In this book, you'll find 100 recipes that cover every aspect of the Big Green Egg. You'll learn how to master the classics, like brisket and pork shoulder, and a few new methods and flavor twists to keep things exciting when you get in a rut. From smoking and grilling to roasting and baking—the recipes in this book will teach you how to do it all.

When I first got my Big Green Egg, I went into it knowing I wanted to master this cooker. So I committed myself to cooking on it every night for 30 days. As hard as that seemed at the start of this project, it was the best decision I made. At the end of the 30-day period, I felt confident lighting the charcoal, controlling temperature, setting up the Big Green Egg for the various styles of cooking it can do, and—most importantly—I gained experience in handling the inevitable issues that arise when cooking with a live-fire grill. From that point on, I was a certified EGGhead, and I am happy to be a member of the wonderful community of EGGheads around the world.

When social media captured everyone's attention in the early 2010s, I was on the forefront of posting creations and recipes cooked on the Big Green Egg. Fast-forward to several years later: Big Green Egg reached out, asking me to join their team of social media influencers from around the globe. I was humbled and dedicated myself to this new venture. I went into it with a passion. I have been fortunate to travel around the United States with Big Green Egg, performing demos at various festivals such as Memphis in May, Hot Luck, Atlanta Food and Wine Festival and many more. I love to teach and learn from the many great cooks in the EGGhead community.

With my background, it made all the sense in the world to write about a subject I know well and love: the Big Green Egg. In this book, you will learn my best tips and tricks for setting up your Big Green Egg and managing its temperature in addition to the numerous recipes. I hope this book inspires you to cook and master the many aspects of the Big Green Egg. Please come find me at the next Big Green Egg festival and say hello!

CHAPTER 1

Getting Started

WITH YOUR
BIG GREEN EGG

When I first got my Big Green Egg in 2009, I was a bit intimidated. I knew I had the skills to be successful on this new grill, as I had been smoking and grilling meat for many years on various other cookers. But when I made the investment in my Big Green Egg, I wanted to make sure that I was going to master its functions and everything it had to offer. As you know, I made a commitment to cook on my Big Green Egg every day for 30 days. That experience cemented my skill set early, galvanizing my love for this new cooker. I am still cooking on it almost every day all these years later. In this section, I will distill my experience into a layperson's terms to help you understand and, better yet, master all the amazing things this cooker can do.

The Big Green Egg really can do it all: smoking, grilling, roasting and baking. With some knowledge, practice and tenacity, you, too, will learn to do all these things with yours. I'll break down each of these functions, outline some of the must-have accessories to get the most out of your Big Green Egg and show you the best ways to set it up for a successful cook.

HOW DOES A BIG GREEN EGG WORK?

First, let's look at the basic design of this grill and how it is optimized for any kind of cooking you plan to do. The setup of the Big Green Egg allows you to move seamlessly between low and slow cooking to high-heat grilling and everything in between. When you learn the basics of each style of cooking, you are then empowered to get creative with the Big Green Egg, adapting your cooking style to any situation.

Ceramic Design

This cooker is made from state-of-the-art ceramic technologies (a combination of high-temperature ceramics, terracotta and crushed lava rock), which provide incredible insulation. This design can withstand temperatures of more than 750°F (399°C) without breaking, even when there are temperature fluctuations produced by the cook opening and closing the grill.

The thick ceramic walls absorb heat and release it back slowly during the long cook, which helps maintain even cooking temperatures. In addition, the ceramic insulation helps manage fuel consumption, so you do not need to reload your fuel—even during a long cook.

Fuel Source

The Big Green Egg is fueled by lump charcoal and not the charcoal briquettes that many other cookers use. Lump charcoal is made from pieces of wood and lumber scraps, whereas briquettes are made mostly from sawdust mixed with additives. The wood used to make lump charcoal is heated in a device, like a kiln, that features low levels of oxygen. This process of heating the wood in a low-oxygen environment ensures it does not burn to ashes, which would make the wood unusable. Lump charcoal is unique because it burns hotter,

allowing you to reach temperatures of 600°F (316°C) or higher. In addition, when used for low and slow cooking (i.e., temperatures between 200 and 275°F [93 and 135°C]), it burns for a much longer time, making it the optimal choice for BBQ. As the wood burns, it does not create as much ash as briquettes. The lack of ash facilitates airflow and helps maintain the fuel source for a long period of time. I have had cooks last longer than 14 hours, yet I didn't have to refuel.

Shape

The oval shape of the Big Green Egg combined with its ceramic insulation creates a hot airstream that circulates around the meat cooking inside. Essentially, you have a live-fire convection oven. The Big Green Egg is designed to cook with the lid closed throughout the cook to ensure you are harnessing the full power of this egg-shaped design and managing the temperature properly.

Airtight Seal

On the Big Green Egg's top and bottom domes you will find a felt material known as the gasket. This material creates an almost airtight seal when the top dome is closed. This important seal enhances heat retention inside the Big Green Egg and prevents moisture from leaving the cooker, which helps maintain the right humidity levels. The combination of this tight seal and the thickness of the ceramic material is second to none at retaining moisture, ensuring your food never dries out.

Heat Shield

For the old-school EGGheads out there, you knew this as the Plate Setter. The current name for this ceramic deflector is the convEGGtor. No matter what you call it, this piece is critical to smoking anything on your Big Green Egg. Basically, the convEGGtor is a ceramic heat shield, protecting your food from the burning charcoal below. This heat shield helps circulate the hot air in and around the dome, creating that charcoal-fueled convection oven effect.

Air Vents

Arguably the most important design features of the Big Green Egg are the air vents on top and bottom, which are meant to manage the amount of heated air moving through the cooking chamber. These vents allow the user to set and manage the cooking temperature as if it were on a sliding scale.

- Top vent (Chimney): The vent on top of your Big Green Egg in combination with the rEGGulator allows you to dial in the cooking temperature accurately. The rEGGulator is the cast-iron cap sitting on the top vent of the Big Green Egg helping to control airflow. I will cover this more on page 16.

- Bottom vent (Draft Door): This is your main air source, the place where the Big Green Egg will take in the oxygen needed to maintain the fire. Knowing how to manage this vent in combination with the top vent is the key to setting the right temperature for smoking and BBQ.

Thermometer

Your Big Green Egg comes with a thermometer that is set about two-thirds up the dome. It is important to keep in mind a couple of things when using the Big Green Egg's thermometer. First, the difference in temperature from the grill grate to the top part of the dome where the thermometer is set can be as much as 50°F (10°C). So if your target temperature is 250°F (121°C), just know the temperature measured at the dome could be 300°F (149°C). When cooking on your Big Green Egg, be aware of this difference and adjust accordingly. For high-heat cooks (e.g., 350°F [177°C] or higher), I do not worry about the temperature variance much—it will not impact what and how you are cooking. But for low and slow cooks, that temperature variance should be considered. Weather and outdoor temperatures also affect the accuracy of the dome's gauge. Over time, the thermometer at the dome will need tuning and adjustments to measure temperature accurately. A great way to monitor temperature in your Big Green Egg is with a digital probe (I like the Flame Boss® 500-WiFi Kamado Smoker Controller Kit). The probe used with this tool is accurate and measures at the grill grate, ensuring that you are measuring the temperature at the optimal location.

Set the bottom vent open only a little bit for low and slow cooking.

Set the bottom vent open wide for grilling.

MUST-HAVE BIG GREEN EGG COMPONENTS AND ACCESSORIES

In my opinion, there are must-have additions to your Big Green Egg setup that take your cooking ability to the next level. If you want to have better command over your setup and cooking environment, the following is my list of add-ons you should have on hand.

Fire Bowl and Divider or Kick Ash Basket System

Whether you purchase the Big Green Egg's Fire Bowl or the Kick Ash Basket, you will be happy with this addition to your Big Green Egg setup. Managing the cleanup and use of your lump charcoal is made much easier with this gear. Use either of these devices to shake loose ash and debris before you light your lump charcoal for the next cook. In addition, if you get the divider for either system, it will turn your Big Green Egg into a two-zone grill with ease.

EGGspander

This accessory from Big Green Egg is a game changer because it allows you to take advantage of all the vertical space inside. The multitier system allows you to cook at the grilling surface and above. In addition, this add-on helps manage your indirect, direct, raised direct and cowboy grilling setup.

Half-Moon Inserts

Having an array of Big Green Egg half-moon inserts on hand helps you take your grilling game to the next level. They fit in and work with the EGGspander system, allowing you to use grill grates in different configurations: (1) use ceramic stones for a two-zone grilling setup; (2) try cast-iron grates for the perfect sear; or (3) use the plancha to turn your Big Green Egg into a flattop grill.

Cast-Iron Accessories

I am a big fan of cooking with cast iron on the Big Green Egg. I feel that Lodge® brand cast iron is the right choice from a price and functionality perspective. Having an array of cast-iron skillets—from 8 to 12 inches (20 to 30 cm)—will cover most of your cooking needs. In addition, having a 5-quart (4.8-L) cast-iron Dutch oven is a great addition to your lineup, as it helps you braise meats and make delicious soups.

Tools to Help Manage Your Fuel Source and Temperature

The fuel source and temperature are variables you must manage for every cook. Here are my recommendations to help you achieve the best results every time you cook on your Big Green Egg:

- Charcoal: For me, the best lump charcoal on the market is made by FOGO. This handpicked wood is sustainably sourced and offers longer-burning coals. You will come to crave the signature Inga wood flavor that comes from El Salvadoran Inga trees.

Getting ready to light the lump charcoal with fire starters in a triangle pattern for a hot and fast cook.

- Fire starters: The next best option after the SpeediLight® fire starters from Big Green Egg is the Looft® Lighter. Their new Looft Lighter X is wireless and very powerful. This battery-powered fire starter has a low-powered blower on it to help create the right fire every time. I have had success using a methylacetylene-propa-diene propane (MAPP) torch to light lump charcoal as well.

- Instant-read thermometer: To be successful on the grill, every pit master needs a good instant-read thermometer. I use the Thermapen® from ThermoWorks. In my view, this is the best digital thermometer on the market.

- Heat-resistant gloves: You need a good set of gloves to protect your hands when cooking in a live-fire environment or handling hot cast-iron cookware. Heat-resistant gloves, made from durable heat-resistant fibers, offer your hands protection from temperatures as high as 500°F (260°C). Big Green Egg has a glove that I like named the EGGmitt® BBQ Glove, though there are many others to choose from that can be purchased online or at your local BBQ store.

KEY TECHNIQUES FOR SMOKING BBQ LIKE A PRO

If you purchased your Big Green Egg for smoked meats, you made the right decision. This grill's design is perfect for low and slow cooks. In this section, I will show you how to set up your Big Green Egg for smoking and how to manage the temperature of the Big Green Egg for long cooks.

How to Set Up Your Big Green Egg for a Long Smoke

When smoking on your Big Green Egg, you need to focus on the "BBQ Zone," which is the temperature range best suited for cooking larger, tougher cuts of meat to BBQ perfection. The temperature range between 200 and 275°F (93 and 135°C) is ideal for breaking down connective tissue, helping turn a large or tough piece of meat into a smoky, tender masterpiece.

In the sections that follow, I will review my method for setting up the charcoal and wood to achieve the BBQ Zone of temperature in your Big Green Egg.

For a low and slow cook: (A) Place three smoke wood chunks on the charcoal in a triangle pattern.

(B) Top off the wood chunks with more charcoal.

Dialing In the Temperature for the BBQ Zone

First, let's explore how to build the optimal fire, place the wood and manage the temperature needed to cook in the BBQ Zone.

To start, make certain to clean your Big Green Egg's Fire Box, Fire Bowl and Fire Grate of old ash, debris and small pieces of lump left from previous cooks. It is essential you have proper airflow between the Big Green Egg's Draft Door and the rEGGgulator sitting on top of the Chimney.

To set up the Big Green Egg for smoking, first place a small amount of lump charcoal in the Fire Box, just enough to cover the Fire Grate (about one-fourth of the total space available). From there, place three or four baseball-sized chunks of smoking wood in the base of the charcoal. Make sure they are spaced apart so they will not all light at the same time.

Once your wood is in place, fill the rest of the Fire Bowl with lump charcoal.

As discussed earlier, you could get up to 12 hours (or more) of cooking time with a full load of lump charcoal in your Big Green Egg. This is achieved with the heat absorbed by the ceramic materials, the tight air seal keeping the oxygen flow controlled and the lump charcoal, which burns more efficiently than other charcoal types.

After your charcoal and wood are in place, it is time to light and manage the fire. If you ask 100 different EGGheads how they light their Big Green Egg, you will certainly get 100 different answers. What works best for me is using my 10 x 10 x 10 method, which I will outline here.

To start, light your fire toward the front of the Fire Bowl closest to the Draft Door below. Leave the Draft Door and the top dome open all the way, and let the fire burn uninterrupted for 10 minutes. In this state, your Big Green Egg is getting the most oxygen possible to create the combustion temperature necessary to produce clean smoke.

Close the rEGGulator 90% to control a low and slow cook.

These adjustments are the big reason why modern Kamado grills are perfect for smoking—you can dial in the exact temperature you desire and know it will stay in place for the duration of the cook.

To keep the temperature stable for smoking, you will want to shut both the rEGGulator and the Draft Door 90 percent of the way (shown in the photo on the left). For the final 10 minutes, manage the vent settings to achieve the desired temperature between 200 and 275°F (93 and 135°C). Making small adjustments to the vents to reach the desired temperature typically takes the full 10 minutes. From here, it is time to start smoking!

Humidity and the Big Green Egg

The most important factor to manage when you are cooking low and slow BBQ on your Big Green Egg is humidity. When I first started smoking meats, I thought the white smoke billowing from the cooker was what gave the meat both color and flavor. I soon learned that I couldn't have been more wrong. The white smoke you see when cooking with wood comes from the carcinogens burning off from the living plant material. That part of the smoke actually leaves an unpleasant acrid taste on your food. What you are looking for is a thin, bluish-gray smoke coming from your cooker. When you see that, you know the fuel source and the wood burning inside are releasing a mixture of oils, liquid droplets and vapors that in turn give your food that distinctive color and flavor.

Next, put your convEGGtor (or two ceramic half-moon inserts if you are using the EGGspander base) and grill grate in place and close the top dome. When you do this, the temperature will drop considerably as the convEGGtor or ceramic inserts will block the burning coals below from the temperature probe in the dome. After the insert is placed, be patient while the temperature begins to rise toward the desired range.

For this stage, you want both the Draft Door and the rEGGgulator fully open, allowing in as much oxygen as possible to ramp up the temperature of your fire. Leave your Big Green Egg in this state for another 10 minutes. When you come back to check, the temperature should be around 250°F (121°C).

Finally, adjust the vents on your Draft Door and your rEGGulator. After you place the convEGGtor in the Big Green Egg, the airflow will start to move around considerably—this creates a convection cooking environment. The air vents allow you to control the airflow as it is drawn in from the bottom and released from the top.

Adding a steam table pan with warm water helps keep the environment humid during a long cook.

The best way to manage proper humidity during your cook is to watch as the pellicle forms on the outside of your meat. The pellicle is a very thin layer that forms on the surface of the meat as the proteins in the meat break down and form polymers. You want the pellicle to be moist to allow the gases, vapors and oils to stick to the outside of the meat and in turn get absorbed by the meat. But you do not want the pellicle to be so wet that the gases, vapors and oils roll right off the surface of the meat. Basically, you will need to watch the outside of the meat as it cooks to see when and where dry spots form and use a spritzer to add a fine mist of moisture to those areas. For long cooks (e.g., brisket) using a ¼ steam table pan full of warm water (pictured above) can be helpful as well.

The good news for Big Green Egg owners is that the Big Green Egg has an airtight ceramic cooking chamber, which keeps food moist by trapping excess moisture released during a cook. Basically, as meat cooks it expresses moisture, which is then turned into the humidity needed for good BBQ—a range of 70 to 80 percent humidity is ideal. This insulated environment keeps external heat and cold from affecting the food inside for the duration of the cook.

GUIDE TO GRILLING

When you are grilling on the Big Green Egg, you have many setup options to consider and use. The goal when grilling food is to expose whatever you are cooking to direct heat in a controlled fashion, so that you have the desired outcome when the cook is finished. Let's review four ways to set up your Big Green Egg for grilling success.

1. Direct

This is the setup your Big Green Egg has right out of the box. The grilling surface is 6 inches (15 cm) or so below the felt line (the place where the dome meets the bottom of the Big Green Egg). There is no ceramic insert between the lighted lump charcoal in the Fire Box and grill grate. This gets you close to the coals but not so close that you have no control. This is the most common setup for grilling on the Big Green Egg.

2. Raised Direct

This is my preferred setup and the one I use to grill food with all the time. In this scenario, you are using the EGGspander base (or, for the old-school EGGheads out there, a Woo from the Ceramic Grill Store) to raise the grilling surface in order to align it with the felt line (the place where the dome meets the bottom of the Big Green Egg). This raised grilling surface allows you greater control over the lighted lump charcoal below, as it is 6 inches (15 cm) higher than the standard setup described in the preceding paragraph. By having the grilling surface farther away from the heat source, you are easily able to manage flare-ups as the meat's fat renders and drips onto the coals below. In addition, since your hands are farther away from the heat source, handling the grilling surface is much easier and more comfortable for you as the cook.

3. Two-Zone Grilling

This setup is essentially spelled out for you in the name. You have one zone setup for direct grilling (the food is directly exposed to the lighted lump charcoal) and the other for indirect grilling (the food is exposed only to ambient heat in the cooking chamber). This setup gives you the most control over grilling food, as you can move the food from being directly exposed to the fire below to a cooler zone, allowing it to bake or roast. This is the perfect setup for reverse searing.

There are two ways to achieve the two-zone grilling setup on the Big Green Egg. The first is using the Fire Box to divide the charcoal into two zones. To do this, you need the Fire Bowl with the divider (XL, 2XL) or the Kick Ash Basket with Adjustable Divider. The second way to achieve two-zone grilling is to use the EGGspander base with a half-moon ceramic insert. This way, you still have two zones—direct and indirect—but the indirect side has more radiant heat coming from below, which is baffled by the ceramic insert. My preference is to use the divider in your Fire Box, as this is a true two-zone setup (i.e., the cool side has no ambient heat coming from below).

4. Cowboy Grilling

This setup puts the grill grate directly over the lighted lump charcoal below. To do this, you need the EGGspander Multi-Level Rack. The top tier of the EGGspander Multi-Level Rack can be turned upside down where it fits perfectly into the notches in the Fire Ring and drops the grill grate to an inch (2.5 cm) or so above the charcoal. This style of cooking is indeed hot and fast, as you need to cook the food for only a minute or two per side. Typically this style of cooking is reserved for big cuts of beef like picanha, tomahawk rib eyes and the like.

Big Green Egg Setup and Temperature Control for Grilling

To set up the Big Green Egg for grilling (including two-zone and cowboy grilling), load your lump charcoal in the Fire Box, filling it about halfway. Now it is time to light your fire and get grilling. Take three SpeediLight fire starters and nestle them in the lump charcoal, forming a triangle with the fire starters. Let's use a clock as a visual reference for SpeediLight distribution: Place one at 12:00, one at 4:00 and one at 8:00. Light the fire starters.

Now, using my 10 x 10 x 10 method, leave the Draft Door and top dome completely open and let the fire burn uninterrupted for 10 minutes. In this state, your Big Green Egg is getting the most oxygen possible to create the combustion temperature necessary to produce clean smoke.

Next, place your grill grate in the Big Green Egg and close the top dome, leaving the top and bottom vents completely open. Let the fire burn like this for another 10 minutes.

At this point, you should be at or near 350°F (177°C) and can now start adjusting the top and bottom vents to stabilize or change the temperature. Typically foods are grilled at a temperature between 400 and 600°F (204 and 316°C), so starting to tune your vents at 350°F (177°C) helps you dial in the right temperature with greater control. Once you are dialed in, you are ready to start grilling!

BAKING AND ROASTING WITH THE BIG GREEN EGG

The most important thing to do in order to bake successfully on your Big Green Egg is to ensure it is clean before you start. When I say clean, I mean clean! The last thing you want your friends and family to taste when eating a pie or a loaf of bread baked on the Big Green Egg is all the BBQ that came before your baked creation. To get your Big Green Egg in the best shape possible to bake, you will need to perform a "clean burn" the day before you plan to do your baking.

The Clean Burn

Fill half of your Big Green Egg Fire Bowl with fresh lump charcoal. Light the lump charcoal, place the convEGGtor and grill grate in place and get the temperature up to a range between 650 and 750°F (343 and 399°C). Once you stabilize the temperature, set a timer for an hour and then leave the grill alone. When the hour is up, shut the top and bottom vents; doing so will allow the Big Green Egg to cool down. When it has cooled, you will find the clean burn has loosened or dissolved all of the grease buildup in your Big Green Egg and on your grill grate and convEGGtor.

Once your Big Green Egg is completely cool, it is time to break out the shop vacuum and a stiff metal spatula. Remove any remaining lump charcoal, the Fire Ring and Fire Box. Using the spatula, scrape off any remaining grease buildup in and around the dome, Fire Box and grate that wasn't dissolved during the clean burn. Thoroughly vacuum up the scrapings with your shop vacuum. After vacuuming all the ash and debris, reassemble your freshly cleaned Big Green Egg.

Baking Setup

Setting up your Big Green Egg for baking is just like setting it up for smoking but with one key difference: You will not use smoking wood of any kind. Simply fill the Fire Bowl as you would for a low and slow cook, light your fire, place the convEGGtor (or two ceramic half-moon inserts if you are using the EGGspander base) and grill grate inside the Big Green Egg and start baking when your desired temperature is reached.

BIG GREEN EGG TROUBLESHOOTING AND MAINTENANCE GUIDE

Many people ask me how to manage temperature in a Big Green Egg, while others wonder how best to clean and maintain it. This section will give you some troubleshooting tips regarding temperature control as well as show you how to properly care for your Big Green Egg.

Tricks to Manage Temperature Control When Things Go Wrong

In this section, I will break down the two most common issues people run into when cooking on the Big Green Egg: First, they cannot get their Big Green Egg hot enough (350°F [177°C] or higher). Second, they need to cool their Big Green Egg down to 250°F (121°C) or lower for smoking. Let's look at what you can do to fix each scenario.

Trouble Getting Your Big Green Egg to 350°F (177°C) or Higher

The best way to fix this is by following the cleaning tips in the section titled "Cleaning and Maintenance" to the right. Obstructed airflow is the top reason your Big Green Egg won't get to 350°F (177°C) or higher. Make sure you do the precook cleaning before you get started on your next cook that requires temps of 350°F (177°C) or higher.

Trouble Getting Your Big Green Egg's Temperature to 250°F (121°C) or Lower for Smoking

Has this happened to you: You have set up your Big Green Egg for a low and slow cook, the temperature gets above 300°F (149°C) and you can't get the temperature lower? Well, this scenario happens all the time, and you may be surprised by the solution. Using heat-resistant gloves, take the convEGGtor (or the EGGspander base and ceramic half-moon inserts) out of the Big Green Egg and top the lighted lump charcoal with unlit lump charcoal. This sounds counterintuitive, but it works by starving the current fire of the needed oxygen it needs to grow. Since the fire can no longer grow, it begins to die down until the unlit charcoal on top ignites. By this time, you have lowered the temperature to your desired range and have adjusted the top and bottom vents to keep it that way for the long cook.

Calibrating the External Temperature Gauge

Before taking the actions below, make sure your Big Green Egg has cooled down and is not hot to the touch. I suggest using a heat-resistant glove for this exercise.

If your external temperature gauge is not reading correctly, it needs to be adjusted. To do this, remove the external temperature gauge from the top dome of your Big Green Egg. Next, carefully boil a pot of water on your stove. Place the stem of the external temperature gauge in the boiling water, being careful not to touch the tip to the bottom of the pot.

After 1 minute in the boiling water, your external temperature gauge should read 212°F (100°C). If it does not read the correct temperature, you need to make small adjustments to correctly set the temperature. Remove the stem from the boiling water, then use a 1-cm wrench to rotate the nut at the top of the stem of your external temperature gauge. Rotating it clockwise will raise the temperature and rotating it counterclockwise will lower it. Continue making small adjustments and checking the temperature in the boiling water until you have set it correctly.

Cleaning and Maintenance

Cleaning your Big Green Egg is something you should do regularly, as it will impact its performance and your ability to manage the temperature for each cook. I divide the task of cleaning into two separate categories: (1) precook cleaning and (2) biannual maintenance cleaning. Let's dig into each one so you can be set up for success.

Important: Make sure to clean your Big Green Egg when it has not been used recently and is cool. You do not want to hurt yourself or cause a fire by cleaning when the Big Green Egg is still hot from your previous cook.

Precook Cleaning

First, think about your prior cook: If it was greasy, you will have dried grease over the remaining lump charcoal, impacting its ability to burn evenly. In addition, the burnt grease will negatively affect the flavor of the food you are cooking now. If your prior cook was greasy, throw out all the lump charcoal (not just the ash and debris) and start with a fresh batch. If you are using lump charcoal from your previous cook, you must clean the old ash and debris to ensure proper airflow management. I suggest using either the Kick Ash Basket or the Big Green Egg's Fire Bowl to make this job much easier. Take your Kick Ash Basket or Fire Bowl and shake all the small bits of ash and debris loose and into a metal garbage can. If you are not using either of those devices, take your Ash Tool and run it through the leftover lump charcoal until the ash and debris fall through the Fire Grate and into the Fire Box below. Then use the Ash Tool to remove the ash and debris through the bottom Draft Door. After all the previous ash and debris have been removed, look at the Fire Grate and make sure nothing is blocking the holes, which would prevent oxygen from reaching the fire.

Biannual Maintenance Cleaning

Twice a year, I will take the Big Green Egg apart by removing the inside components (the cooking grid, Fire Ring, Fire Grate and Fire Box) and clean all the debris, ash and fallen pieces of lump charcoal that have accumulated inside. Note that it helps to do a clean burn before you do this: Heat your Big Green Egg to 600°F (316°C) and let it run at that temperature for an hour. This process will clean your cooking grid, convEGGtor, Fire Ring, Fire Grate and Fire Box by burning grease and buildup left from previous cooks.

After the clean burn, allow the Big Green Egg to completely cool down, then remove the components mentioned in the preceding paragraph. Use a shop vacuum to remove all the ash, debris and so on from the bottom of your Big Green Egg. In addition, this is a good time to check the gaskets on the top and bottom domes. The gaskets last two or three years with normal use, so you shouldn't have to change them often. However, this biannual check is the right time to make that decision. Finally, this is the time to check that all the bolts are tightened on the bands holding your Big Green Egg together. Over time the bolts loosen and in turn, the bottom and top domes become misaligned. To prevent this, a semiannual tightening of the bolts should be done.

WHERE TO GO FROM HERE

That's it in a nutshell, my friends! You have all the knowledge you need to cook the 100 recipes in this book. For each recipe, I will refer to this chapter of the book so you can refresh your memory on exactly how to set up the Big Green Egg for the cook. I hope you find as much joy in cooking with this grill as I do!

CHAPTER 2

The Smoke Show

MUST-HAVE LOW AND SLOW BBQ RECIPES

Let's face it—you bought the Big Green Egg to smoke all your BBQ favorites. Well, this chapter has it all: everything from the classics, such as pulled pork and brisket, to some new and exciting recipes. If you are looking to master the art of BBQ on your Big Green Egg, this chapter is the place to start!

FEEDS: 20 people

APPROXIMATE COOK TIME:
10–16 hours

BIG GREEN EGG SETUP:
Indirect

TOOLS AND ACCESSORIES:
convEGGtor, ¼ steam
table pan, pink butcher
paper, full-sized aluminum
pan, plastic wrap, clean
empty cooler and old
towel

SUGGESTED WOOD TYPE:
Oak or hickory chunks

BRISKET

12–15-lb (5.4–6.8-kg) whole
packer brisket

1 tbsp (15 ml) yellow mustard

1 cup (240 ml) beef broth

DRY RUB

½ cup (48 g) ground black
pepper (ideally 16 mesh)

¼ cup (18 g) Lawry's®
Seasoned Salt

¼ cup (72 g) kosher salt

The BBQ Buddha's Midnight Brisket

This perfect-every-time recipe will help you get a delicious brisket done while you are sleeping. If you time it correctly, you will be able to wake up and pick up where you left off the night before. This recipe is perfect if you want to serve your brisket for lunch or dinner the following day. Note that this recipe is just a suggested timeline and can be affected by the size of the brisket you are cooking.

10 P.M.- PREPARING THE MEAT

Trim the fat cap of the brisket down to ¼ inch (6 mm). Trim the large chunk of hard fat that sits between the point and flat muscles on the meat side of the brisket. Trim the sides and ends to be uniform in shape.

Lightly slather the mustard across the entire surface of the brisket—the mustard will help the spices adhere to the brisket. In a shaker or small bowl, mix together all of the ingredients for the dry rub. Now, shake the spice mix evenly across all the surfaces of the brisket, or—if you have made the dry rub in a bowl—use your hand to sprinkle the dry rub evenly across the meat. (Note that you may not use all the seasoning and can save a little to add to the brisket when you wrap it.) Let the meat sit at room temperature for at least 1 hour before putting it on the smoker. This allows the meat to start cooking faster, since it will be at a lower temperature. If you put a large cut of meat like this in the smoker when the meat is still cold, it will add at least an hour to your total cook time.

11 P.M.- SETTING UP THE GRILL

Load the Big Green Egg with natural lump charcoal and mix in four chunks of oak or hickory wood with the lump charcoal (as described on page 16). Now light the charcoal and preheat the Big Green Egg to 225°F (107°C), using the convEGGtor for indirect grilling.

This cook is an ideal opportunity to use a smoker and BBQ temperature control system like the EGG Genius or the Flame Boss 500-WiFi Kamado Smoker Controller Kit. This incredible tool uses Wi-Fi to monitor and maintain the temperature inside your Big Green Egg, and it will alert you if the temperature deviates more than a set amount. This tool is essential to your getting a good night's sleep during this cook.

(continued)

When the Big Green Egg has preheated and you are ready to put the brisket inside, place a ¼ steam table pan of warm water on top of the grill grate to help introduce more humidity to this long cook.

12 A.M.– PUTTING THE MEAT ON THE GRILL

Once the temperature is stable at 225°F (107°C) and you see the smoke turn from white to bluish gray, it is time to put your meat inside the Big Green Egg. Place the brisket fat side down on the grill grate. The fat cap renders slowly during the long cook and will act as a barrier between the meat and the heat source, preventing the surface area from drying out. After the meat is on, place the meat probe from your Wi-Fi smoker controller and temperature management system into the flat side of the brisket. Make sure you do not place it so far down in the brisket that the probe is sticking into the fat separating the point and the flat. You want the probe firmly in the flat muscle of the brisket to get accurate results. Once the probe is in place and the temperature is stable, go to sleep, setting your alarm for 6:00 a.m. the next day.

6 A.M.– WAKING UP AND MANAGING THE STALL

When you wake up, check your data from the Wi-Fi smoker controller and temperature management system. In my experience, the brisket will be in the middle or near the end of the "stall," the period in which the internal temperature of the brisket stalls between 150 and 165°F (66 and 74°C).

Once the brisket's internal temperature is at 165°F (74°C) and its bark is a dark mahogany color, it is time to take it off the smoker and wrap it.

6 TO 7 A.M.– WRAPPING YOUR BRISKET

At this point, you have the choice to wrap the brisket in aluminum foil or pink butcher paper. While I have had success with both methods, I usually wrap my brisket in butcher paper, as it gives you an advantage with bark formation.

Before you remove the brisket from the Big Green Egg, prepare two pieces of butcher paper that are each roughly 30 inches (75 cm) long. Overlap them so that you can place the brisket on the paper.

Carefully remove the brisket from the Big Green Egg and place it about one-third of the way up the overlapping pieces of butcher paper. Spray the brisket one more time with the spritz bottle of water you have been using during this cook. Add a few shakes of the dry rub to the surface of the meat. Wrap the brisket in the butcher paper: Fold the end of the butcher paper closest to you up and over the top of the brisket, then fold the sides up on the right and left (like you are making a burrito) and then roll the brisket away from you.

Pour the broth in the bottom of a full-sized aluminum pan. Then place the wrapped brisket in the pan. Place the pan in the Big Green Egg and let the meat cook until it is done.

10 A.M. TO 12 P.M.– CHECKING YOUR BRISKET FOR DONENESS

From this point on, the cook is a waiting game—the brisket will rise in temperature from 165°F (74°C) to somewhere between 190 and 210°F (88 and 99°C). Here are the doneness cues to look for, along with the actions to take, so that you will know when the brisket is ready to come off the Big Green Egg.

Temperature: Brisket is two muscles joined together with a thick layer of fat. One muscle is large and fatty while the other is long, flat and lean. Both muscles will not reach the same temperature at the same time, so I like to take my cues from the flat as that is the hardest part to get right. Once your flat starts measuring somewhere between 190 and 210°F (88 and 99°C), you are ready to move on to the final test to determine if the brisket is done.

The best way to take the brisket's temperature is to poke your probe right through the butcher paper. You can alternatively pull the aluminum pan out of the cooker and crack the butcher paper, revealing the brisket to check for both visual and textural cues. In addition, I check the temperature every 30 minutes once the internal temperature measures between 190 and 210°F (88 and 99°C) to ensure I do not overcook it, which would turn the brisket to lifeless shredded beef.

Feel: Now that your brisket's flat is measuring between 190 and 210°F (88 and 99°C), use the thermometer probe to check the flat and point for tenderness. You want the thermometer to go in and out of the brisket with little to no resistance. Think of it like poking a ziplock bag that contains warm mashed potatoes. The probe needs to slide in and out with ease. If it doesn't, leave the brisket in your Big Green Egg and continue checking it every 30 minutes, until that ease of movement is what you feel when taking the temperature.

Once you have decided the brisket is at the proper tenderness, you are done but you are not ready to eat yet. Carefully remove the pan with the brisket from the Big Green Egg and get ready for the resting step.

12 TO 2 P.M. – RESTING

Now that the brisket is off the Big Green Egg, take the brisket out of the aluminum pan, pour out the beef stock and drippings from the brisket so that the pan is empty and open the butcher paper wrap slightly at one of the seams, allowing the heat and steam to escape. Put the partially wrapped brisket back in the aluminum pan (to catch any drippings), and let the brisket sit at room temperature until the brisket's internal temperature drops to 165°F (74°C)—this usually takes 30 minutes. This step stops the carryover cooking and brings the temperature of the brisket to a place that is optimal for resting.

Now, take the brisket out of the aluminum pan, tightly wrapping it in the butcher paper again by closing that exposed seam and place it on a cutting board or other clean work surface. Wrap it in plastic wrap, then wrap an old towel around the plastic wrap. Place the fully wrapped brisket in an empty cooler for at least 2 hours and up to 4 hours. This resting stage is a key step in getting your brisket as juicy as possible.

The reason you rest a wrapped brisket for 2 to 4 hours is that the longer the brisket rests, the more the rendered fat and collagen settle and get reabsorbed into the muscle fibers as the meat cools and relaxes. This enables you to serve your dinner guests the juiciest brisket ever. The sweet spot for most people is 2 hours, but you can wait an extra 2 hours if that accommodates your serving time. You can rest the meat longer, but I feel the texture of the brisket suffers some if it rests more than 4 hours.

2 TO 4 P.M. – SLICING AND SERVING

Finally, when you are ready to serve, take the brisket out of the cooler. Remove the wrapping and place the brisket on a cutting board. Separate the point from the flat by cutting through the deckle (the fatty layer between each muscle). Now slice the flat into pencil-thin slices. The point can be cubed for burnt ends or sliced against the grain for juicy, fatty slices of brisket deliciousness.

FEEDS: 2–4 people

APPROXIMATE COOK TIME:
5 hours

BIG GREEN EGG SETUP:
Indirect

SUGGESTED WOOD TYPE:
Oak or hickory chunks

TOOLS AND ACCESSORIES:
convEGGtor, 5-quart (4.8-L)
cast-iron Dutch oven

4–5-lb (1.8–2.3-kg) chuck
roast

2 tbsp (24 g) BBQ beef rub (I
used Dizzy Pig® Cow Lick
Spicy Beef Rub)

2 tbsp (30 ml) olive oil

1 yellow onion, diced

2 carrots, peeled and diced

2 ribs celery, diced into
medium pieces

3 cloves garlic, minced

2 (8-oz [240-ml]) cans Bloody
Mary mix (I used Zing Zang®)

4 cups (960 ml) beef stock

2 dried bay leaves

Chuck Roast with Bloody Mary Braise

This is one of my favorite recipes to cook during the winter. Braising the smoked beef in Bloody Mary mix creates the foundation for this recipe. The smoked chuck roast adds such depth of flavor to the braise that you'll wish you had made more. When you are eating this on a cold winter's night, smile—then send me a thank-you note!

Load the Big Green Egg with natural lump charcoal and mix in three chunks of oak or hickory wood with the lump charcoal (as described on page 16). Now light the charcoal and preheat the Big Green Egg to 250°F (121°C), using the convEGGtor for indirect grilling.

Remove the chuck roast from the packaging and season it liberally with the BBQ beef rub. When the Big Green Egg has preheated and the smoke is light gray in color, place your chuck roast inside and let it smoke, undisturbed, for 2 hours. While the roast is smoking, prepare the rest of your ingredients.

When the chuck roast has smoked for 2 hours, remove the roast from the Big Green Egg and let it rest. Place a 5-quart (4.8-L) cast-iron Dutch oven in the Big Green Egg and raise the temperature to 350°F (177°C). Use heat-resistant gloves for this portion of the cook to protect your hands from the heat.

When the Big Green Egg has preheated, add the olive oil to the Dutch oven. Then add the onion, carrots and celery. Let the vegetables cook for 2 to 3 minutes, stirring them occasionally, until they are soft. Add the garlic and cook the mixture for 1 to 2 minutes, until the garlic is fragrant.

Next, deglaze the Dutch oven with the Bloody Mary mix. Add the beef stock, bay leaves and smoked chuck roast. Cover the Dutch oven with its lid and let the chuck roast cook for 2 hours.

At this point, remove and discard the bay leaves. Remove the vegetables with a slotted spoon and transfer them along with a little of the braising liquid to a blender. Pulse the mixture until a thick purée forms. Add the purée to the braising liquid in the Dutch oven, stirring to combine. Let the thickened liquid and chuck roast cook for 30 to 60 minutes. When the smoked chuck roast is fork-tender and shreds easily, it is done.

Remove the Dutch oven from the Big Green Egg, shred the beef and serve it with your favorite side dish.

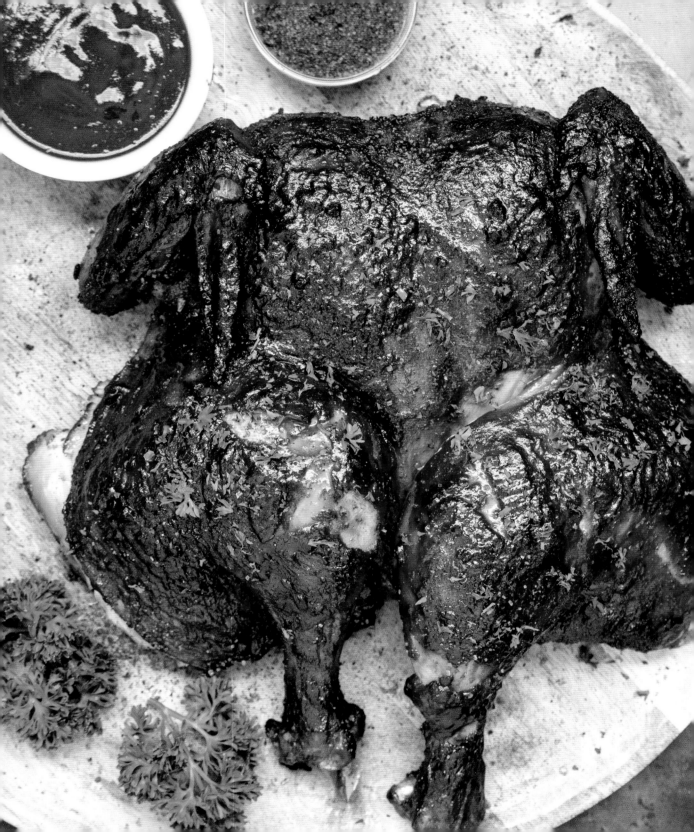

Smoked Spatchcock Chicken

Smoked chicken is one of my favorite things to make. If left alone in the kitchen, I tend to eat more of the whole chicken than I care to admit. Spatchcocking the chicken allows the breast and thighs to cook evenly so everything finishes at the same time and nothing gets dried out or overcooked. This recipe delivers a beautifully smoked bird accented with a tangy BBQ sauce that will most assuredly please your dinner guests.

FEEDS: 2–4 people

APPROXIMATE COOK TIME: 2 hours

BIG GREEN EGG SETUP: Indirect

SUGGESTED WOOD TYPE: Apple or cherry chunks

TOOLS AND ACCESSORIES: convEGGtor

TANGY BBQ SAUCE

2 tbsp (30 ml) olive oil

¼ cup (40 g) finely diced yellow onion

3 cloves garlic, minced

2 cups (480 ml) ketchup

⅓ cup (73 g) brown sugar

⅓ cup (80 ml) molasses

1 tbsp (15 ml) apple cider vinegar

1 tbsp (15 ml) distilled white vinegar

1 tbsp (16 g) tomato paste

1 tbsp (15 ml) Worcestershire sauce

1 tsp chili powder

1 tsp dry mustard

½ tsp cayenne

½ tsp smoked paprika

1 tsp kosher salt

Ground black pepper, to taste

Load the Big Green Egg with natural lump charcoal and mix in three chunks of apple or cherry wood with the lump charcoal (as described on page 16). Next, light the charcoal and preheat the Big Green Egg to 225°F (107°C), using the convEGGtor for indirect grilling.

While the Big Green Egg is preheating, make the tangy BBQ sauce. Using your stove, heat the olive oil in a medium saucepan over medium heat. Add the onion and garlic. Sauté them for 2 to 3 minutes, until they are soft and fragrant. Add the remaining ingredients for the BBQ sauce and reduce the heat to low. Simmer the sauce for 20 to 30 minutes, then use an immersion blender to blend the ingredients until the BBQ sauce is smooth. Set the sauce aside.

(continued)

Smoked Spatchcock Chicken (continued)

DRY RUB

¼ cup (55 g) brown sugar

1 tbsp (18 g) kosher salt

1 tbsp (9 g) chili powder

1 tbsp (7 g) smoked paprika

2 tsp (6 g) garlic powder

2 tsp (6 g) onion powder

¼ tsp ground cumin

CHICKEN

1 (3–4-lb [1.6–1.8-kg]) whole fryer chicken

2 tbsp (30 ml) mayonnaise

While the sauce is simmering and the Big Green Egg is still preheating, mix together all of the ingredients for the dry rub in a shaker or small bowl. You'll only need 2 to 3 tablespoons (24 to 36 g) of dry rub for the chicken, so store the leftover rub in an airtight container for up to 6 months.

To spatchcock the chicken, first cut the backbone out of the chicken using a sharp knife or kitchen shears. Clean up and remove any of the ribs that are still in place. To flatten the bird, place the chicken breast side up, then press down hard with your hands until you hear the breastplate pop. Trim the bird of extra skin.

Rub the chicken all over with the mayonnaise and then coat it with the dry rub. The mayonnaise acts as a binder for the dry rub and helps the skin crisp up as it smokes low and slow. When the Big Green Egg is steady at 225°F (107°C) and the smoke is a light gray color, it is time to place your chicken inside. For this cook, I highly recommend using a remote thermometer to monitor the internal temperature of the chicken while it smokes.

Let the bird smoke undisturbed for 2 hours, until the internal temperature of the breast reaches 150°F (66°C). At that time slather, the smoked chicken with ½ cup (120 ml) of the tangy BBQ sauce, reserving the rest for serving. Let the chicken continue cooking until the internal temperature measures 165°F (74°C) in the breast.

Remove the chicken from the Big Green Egg, carve it and serve it with the reserved BBQ sauce.

FEEDS: 2–4 people

APPROXIMATE COOK TIME:
4–5 hours

BIG GREEN EGG SETUP:
Indirect

SUGGESTED WOOD TYPE:
Hickory or apple chunks

TOOLS AND ACCESSORIES:
convEGGtor

SMOKED SPARERIBS

1 rack of Saint Louis–cut spareribs

2 tbsp (36 g) kosher salt

2 tbsp (12 g) ground black pepper (ideally 16 mesh)

2 tbsp (14 g) paprika

1 tsp yellow mustard

Saint Louis–Style Spareribs with Dr Pepper BBQ Sauce

By far, my favorite soda is Dr Pepper®. So it was only natural that, when I was creating the BBQ sauce for this recipe, I went right for my favorite soda as the star ingredient. This recipe shows you how to smoke a Saint Louis–style cut of spareribs. I use the "Texas crutch" in this recipe: wrapping the ribs mid-cook. At competitions, a professional BBQer is judged on the meat NOT falling off the bone. A common problem with wrapping ribs for too long is that they get too soft and fall off the bone. If you do not want that end result, then this recipe will help. Just a short time in foil will help break down connective tissue and deliver ribs that are tender but do not fall off the bone.

Load the Big Green Egg with natural lump charcoal and mix in three chunks of hickory or apple wood with the lump charcoal (as described on page 16). Now light the charcoal and preheat the Big Green Egg to 225°F (107°C), using the convEGGtor for indirect grilling.

Take the spareribs out of the refrigerator 1 hour before you plan to smoke them. Remove the membrane from the bone side of the spareribs and trim any excess fat from the meat side. Mix together the salt, pepper and paprika to make the rub. Slather the ribs with the yellow mustard and sprinkle the rub on both sides of the ribs.

When the Big Green Egg is stable at 225°F (107°C) and the smoke is light gray in color, place the rack of spareribs bone side down in your Big Green Egg. Let the ribs cook undisturbed for 3 hours. This will allow the pellicle to form and the ribs to take on the flavor of the smoldering wood.

(continued)

Saint Louis–Style Spareribs with Dr Pepper BBQ Sauce (continued)

DR PEPPER BBQ SAUCE

1 (12-oz [360-ml]) can Dr Pepper

2 tbsp (30 ml) olive oil

¼ cup (24 g) minced onion

3 cloves garlic, minced

2 cups (480 ml) ketchup

¼ cup (55 g) brown sugar

1 tbsp (15 ml) apple cider vinegar

1 tbsp (16 g) tomato paste

1 tbsp (15 ml) Worcestershire sauce

2 tsp (6 g) onion powder

2 tsp (6 g) chili powder

1 tsp paprika

Ground black pepper, to taste

FOIL PACKET

2 tbsp (28 g) butter, cut into equal pieces

2 tbsp (30 ml) honey

¼ cup (60 ml) apple juice

While the ribs are smoking, make the Dr Pepper BBQ sauce. Pour the Dr Pepper into a small saucepan. Bring the soda to a boil over high heat, and then reduce the heat to medium-low and bring the soda to a simmer. Allow the Dr Pepper to reduce for approximately 10 minutes, stirring it occasionally. Remove the saucepan from the heat and set it aside.

Heat the olive oil in a medium saucepan over medium heat. Add the onion and sauté it for 2 to 3 minutes, until it has browned slightly. Add the remaining ingredients for the sauce, including the Dr Pepper reduction. Mix the ingredients together thoroughly, reduce the heat to medium-low and simmer the mixture for 20 minutes. Use an immersion blender to blend into a smooth sauce to use on your ribs. Alternatively, carefully transfer the mixture to a countertop blender and blend until the sauce is smooth, then pour it back into the saucepan. If you like, you can add some reserved drippings from the smoked spareribs to add some fatty, rich flavor to this BBQ sauce.

At the 3-hour mark, place the pieces of butter on a sheet of aluminum foil. Pull the ribs out of the Big Green Egg and place them meat side down on top of the butter and drizzle with the honey. Fold the edges of the foil to create a lip all the way around, and then pour ¼ cup (60 ml) of the apple juice to the foil packet you have just created. Now wrap the ribs up in the foil, and then wrap the packet in foil again to ensure the ribs are sealed well. Place the packet in the Big Green Egg and let the ribs cook this way for 1 hour.

Carefully remove the ribs from the foil packet and glaze them with some of the Dr Pepper BBQ sauce. Put the ribs back in the Big Green Egg and let them cook for 30 minutes to set the glaze. Pull the ribs from the Big Green Egg and let them rest for 10 minutes. Slice the ribs and serve them with the remaining BBQ sauce and lots of napkins.

APPROXIMATE COOK TIME:
10–11 hours

BIG GREEN EGG SETUP:
Indirect

SUGGESTED WOOD TYPE:
Hickory chunks

TOOLS AND ACCESSORIES:
convEGGtor

DRY RUB

¼ cup (55 g) brown sugar

¼ cup (28 g) paprika

3 tbsp (54 g) kosher salt

2 tbsp (12 g) ground black pepper (ideally 16 mesh)

2 tbsp (12 g) ground cumin

2 tbsp (18 g) chili powder

1 tbsp (6 g) cayenne

2 tsp (4 g) dry mustard

PORK SHOULDER

1 (8-lb [3.6-kg]) bone-in pork shoulder

2 tbsp (30 ml) yellow mustard

SPRITZ

½ cup (120 ml) apple juice

½ cup (120 ml) apple cider vinegar

½ tsp hot sauce

½ tsp Worcestershire sauce

Bone–In Pork Shoulder

Smoked bone-in pork shoulder (or Boston butt) is one of the easiest things to try when learning how to smoke meat and create delicious BBQ. This large cut of fatty meat is very forgiving and helps you learn without risking too much in the way of time or money. Make sure to find a bone-in pork shoulder, as the bone will help the meat cook more evenly.

Load the Big Green Egg with natural lump charcoal and mix in four chunks of hickory wood with the lump charcoal (as described on page 16). Now light the charcoal and preheat the Big Green Egg to 250°F (121°C), using the convEGGtor for indirect grilling. While the Big Green Egg is preheating, mix together all of the ingredients for the dry rub in a shaker or small bowl. You will need only 2 to 4 tablespoons (24 to 48 g) of the rub for this recipe; the rest can be placed in an airtight container and stored for 2 weeks to use with other pork dishes.

Take the pork shoulder out of the refrigerator at least 1 hour before placing it on your Big Green Egg. If the Big Green Egg is at temperature before the hour is up, it is okay to put the pork in sooner, though it may take a little longer to cook as the meat's core temperature is lower. To prep the pork shoulder, cut a crosshatch pattern on the fat cap of the meat. Slather the pork with the yellow mustard, and then season it with your dry rub, generously covering the whole pork shoulder.

Once the Big Green Egg is stable at 250°F (121°C) and the smoke is light gray in color, put your pork in and let it cook undisturbed for 3 hours. While the pork shoulder is smoking away, mix together all of ingredients for the spritz, and then pour the spritz into a spray bottle.

After the shoulder has been cooking for 3 hours, start spritzing the pork shoulder every hour until the internal temperature measures 165°F (74°C)—this usually takes about 5 hours.

When your pork shoulder measures 165°F (74°C) internally and the bark is set, take your pork off the Big Green Egg and double wrap it in aluminum foil. Put the wrapped pork shoulder back on the Big Green Egg, bump up the temperature to 275°F (135°C) and let the pork cook for 2 to 3 hours, until the internal temperature measures 204°F (96°C) and the meat is probe-tender (i.e., when you insert your digital thermometer probe into the meat, the probe should slide in and out as if you were poking a plastic bag full of warm butter).

When the pork shoulder is ready, take it off the Big Green Egg and let it rest at room temperature for 1 hour before pulling the meat.

FEEDS: 2–4 people

APPROXIMATE COOK TIME:
4–5 hours

BIG GREEN EGG SETUP:
Indirect

SUGGESTED WOOD TYPE:
Hickory or apple chunks

TOOLS AND ACCESSORIES:
convEGGtor

RIBS

1 rack of baby back ribs

1 tsp yellow mustard

1 tbsp (18 g) kosher salt

1 tbsp (6 g) black pepper

1 tbsp (7 g) paprika

1 tbsp (14 g) brown sugar

SPRITZ

1 cup (240 ml) apple juice

1 cup (240 ml) apple cider vinegar

HOMESTYLE BBQ SAUCE

2 tbsp (30 ml) olive oil

½ yellow onion, diced

3 cloves garlic, minced

2 cups (480 ml) ketchup

⅓ cup (73 g) brown sugar

¼ cup (60 ml) apple cider vinegar

1 tbsp (16 g) tomato paste

1 tbsp (15 ml) Worcestershire sauce

1 tsp dry mustard

1 tsp hot sauce

1 tsp smoked paprika

Ground black pepper, to taste

Baby Back Ribs with Homestyle BBQ Sauce

I love smoking baby back ribs, as they cook faster than spareribs and typically have more meat on the bones. Nothing beats a classic rack of smoked baby back ribs glazed with a homestyle BBQ sauce. The combination of smoky and sweet that permeates this rack of ribs is so good—this recipe is one I cook often for friends and family.

Load the Big Green Egg with natural lump charcoal and mix in three chunks of hickory or apple wood with the lump charcoal (as described on page 16). Now light the charcoal and preheat the Big Green Egg to 250°F (121°C), using the convEGGtor for indirect grilling.

Trim the ribs of the skirt, excess fat and membrane. Next, slather the ribs with the yellow mustard. In a small bowl, mix together the salt, pepper, paprika and brown sugar. Sprinkle the mixture evenly over the ribs, covering the surface of the meat. Let the ribs sit at room temperature while your Big Green Egg is preheating.

When the Big Green Egg is stable at 250°F (121°C) and the smoke is light gray in color, place the ribs inside, bone side down. Let the ribs smoke undisturbed for 2 hours. Meanwhile, make the spritz by combining the apple juice and apple cider vinegar in a spray bottle. (You will likely have spritz left over after this cook; extra can be stored in the fridge for 2 weeks.) After 2 hours, spritz the ribs with the mixture every 45 minutes as the ribs continue smoking.

To make the homestyle BBQ sauce, heat a medium saucepan over medium heat and add the olive oil. When the oil is shimmering, add the onion and sauté it for 2 to 3 minutes, stirring it frequently. Add the garlic and cook the mixture for 1 minute. Add the remaining ingredients for the sauce, mixing them together well, and bring the sauce to a low boil. Reduce the heat to medium-low and allow the BBQ sauce to simmer for 30 minutes. Use an immersion blender to blend the BBQ sauce and create a thinner consistency. Set the sauce aside.

At the 4-hour mark, check the ribs for doneness. When you see the bones sticking out ¾ inch (2 cm), they measure 200°F (93°C) and they bend without breaking, the ribs are finished cooking. When the ribs reach this point, evenly spread the BBQ sauce on the rack of ribs and cook them for 30 minutes to set the sauce. Pull the ribs from the Big Green Egg and slice them.

FEEDS: 10–12 people

APPROXIMATE COOK TIME:
10–13 hours

BIG GREEN EGG SETUP:
Indirect

SUGGESTED WOOD TYPE:
Hickory or oak chunks

TOOLS AND ACCESSORIES:
convEGGtor, pink
butcher paper, half-sized
aluminum pan

BRISKET POINT

1 (6–8-lb [2.7–3.6-kg]) brisket
point

1 tbsp (15 ml) hot sauce (such
as Cholula®)

1 cup (240 ml) Big Green Egg
Sweet and Smoky Kansas
City Style Barbecue Sauce

½ cup (110 g) dark brown
sugar

4 tbsp (56 g) butter, divided
into small pats

BEEF RUB

2 tsp (12 g) kosher salt

2 tsp (4 g) coarsely ground
black pepper

2 tsp (6 g) garlic powder

SPRITZ

½ cup (120 ml) apple cider
vinegar

½ cup (120 ml) water

1 tsp Worcestershire sauce

1 tsp hot sauce

Brisket Burnt Ends

This dish was made famous in Texas BBQ joints as a bite the pit masters would hand out while customers were waiting in line to be served. Typically, this is the actual burnt ends from the point muscle of a brisket that are trimmed off after the long smoke. Well, you can take the whole brisket point and cube it to make this dish and get many more bites than just one or two. If you can find a butcher to sell you just the brisket point, perfect. If not, you can separate the brisket point from the flat before the cook and cube the point for the burnt ends, reserving the flat for another cook (like the Smoked Brisket Flat recipe on page 80).

Load the Big Green Egg with natural lump charcoal and mix in three chunks of hickory or oak wood with the lump charcoal (as described on page 16). Now light the charcoal and preheat the Big Green Egg to 250°F (121°C), using the convEGGtor for indirect grilling.

Trim up your brisket point by removing any remaining hard fat and trimming the top fat cap until it is ¼ inch (6 mm) thick.

In a small bowl, mix together all of the ingredients for the beef rub. Slather the brisket point with the hot sauce, and then generously season all sides of the meat with the beef rub.

Once the Big Green Egg is stable at 250°F (121°C) and the smoke is light blue in color, place the seasoned brisket point on your Big Green Egg, close the lid and smoke the meat for 3 hours. During this time, mix together all of the ingredients for the spritz in a spray bottle. After the first 3 hours, spritz the brisket point and continue smoking it, spritzing it every hour, until the internal temperature of the meat reaches 165 to 170°F (74 and 77°C). This step typically takes 6 to 8 hours, depending on the size and thickness of the meat.

Once the bark is set and your brisket point's internal temperature reaches 165 to 170°F (74 and 77°C), wrap the meat tightly in pink butcher paper and return it to the Big Green Egg. Smoke the wrapped brisket point until its internal temperature reaches 185 to 195°F (85 and 91°C), which typically takes another 3 hours. Once the beef is at temperature, transfer it to a cutting board.

If you are starting with a whole packer brisket, separate the point from the flat by running a knife through the vein of hard white fat between the two muscles. Then proceed with trimming the brisket point as explained in the directions.

Unwrap the brisket point from the butcher paper, draining any liquid from the paper into a half-sized aluminum pan. Cut the brisket point into cubes that are about 1½ inches (4 cm) thick. Transfer the cubes to the aluminum pan and toss them with the BBQ sauce and brown sugar. Top them with the butter.

Set the uncovered pan of burnt ends back on the Big Green Egg and close the lid. Smoke the meat at 250°F (121°C) for 1 to 2 hours, or until the burnt ends have absorbed the BBQ sauce and are caramelized on all sides. Remove the burnt ends from the Big Green Egg and serve them.

FEEDS: 4 people

APPROXIMATE COOK TIME: 8–10 hours

BIG GREEN EGG SETUP: Indirect

SUGGESTED WOOD TYPE: Hickory or oak chunks

TOOLS AND ACCESSORIES: convEGGtor, ¼ steam table pan

BEEF RUB

2 tbsp (36 g) kosher salt

2 tbsp (12 g) ground black pepper (ideally 16 mesh)

2 tbsp (18 g) garlic powder

RIBS

1 (4-bone, 4–5-lb [1.8–2.3-kg]) section beef chuck ribs

2 tbsp (30 ml) hot sauce (such as Cholula®)

SPRITZ

1 cup (240 ml) apple cider vinegar

1 cup (240 ml) water

¼–½ tsp Worcestershire sauce

¼–½ tsp hot sauce

Smoked Wagyu Beef Short Ribs

Beef short ribs are a cut of meat from the cow's lower rib cage, behind the brisket. This is why beef short ribs are referred to as "brisket on a stick." As a result of its location, the meat is well marbled with lots of connective tissue. I like to smoke beef ribs without wrapping them, so that the meat stays on the bone. Wrapping ribs not only helps them cook faster but also steams them, making them more tender. When you choose not to wrap ribs, the cook will take a little longer but the meat will not fall off the bone.

Load the Big Green Egg with natural lump charcoal and mix in three chunks of hickory or oak wood with the lump charcoal (as described on page 16). Now light the charcoal and preheat the Big Green Egg to 250°F (121°C), using the convEGGtor for indirect grilling.

While the Big Green Egg is preheating, mix together all of the ingredients for the beef rub. Cover the ribs with the hot sauce and season the ribs on all sides with the beef rub. Let the ribs sit at room temperature until your Big Green Egg is done preheating.

Once the Big Green Egg is stable at 250°F (121°C) and the smoke is light blue in color, place the seasoned beef ribs inside and allow them to smoke for 3 hours. To help manage the humidity, I like to put a ¼ steam table pan filled with warm water in the Big Green Egg with the ribs while they smoke.

While the ribs are smoking, mix together all of the ingredients for the spritz in a small bowl. For the spritz in a small bowl. Pour the spritz into a spray bottle. After the ribs have been in the smoke for 3 hours, start spritzing the ribs every 45 to 60 minutes. Continue smoking until the ribs have reached an internal temperature of 204°F (96°C) and are probe-tender. This cook usually takes 8 to 10 hours total, but—as with brisket—every rack of beef ribs is different and that fact can impact the cooking time.

When your beef ribs hit the final temperature of 204°F (96°C) and are probe-tender, remove the ribs from the Big Green Egg, wrap them in aluminum foil and allow them to rest in an insulated cooler for at least 1 hour before slicing them.

FEEDS: 6–8 people

APPROXIMATE COOK TIME: 3–4 hours

BIG GREEN EGG SETUP: Indirect

SUGGESTED WOOD TYPE: Hickory or apple chunks

TOOLS AND ACCESSORIES: ConvEGGtor, wire baking rack, half-sized aluminum pan

DRY RUB

2 tbsp (36 g) kosher salt

2 tbsp (12 g) ground black pepper (ideally 16 mesh)

2 tbsp (14 g) paprika

2 tbsp (28 g) brown sugar

PORK BELLY

10 lb (4.5 kg) pork belly, skinned and cut into 1"(2.5-cm) cubes

1 tbsp (15 ml) yellow mustard

½ cup (110 g) brown sugar

1 tbsp (15 ml) honey

1 stick butter, cut into pats

Pork Belly Burnt Ends with Bourbon BBQ Sauce

This dish is pork's answer to brisket burnt ends, which are a Texas BBQ staple. Instead of using a cubed brisket point, this recipe calls for cubed skinless pork belly. After making this dish and serving it to your guests, you will know why it is nicknamed pork candy!

Load the Big Green Egg with natural lump charcoal and mix in three chunks of hickory or apple wood with the lump charcoal (as described on page 16). Now light the charcoal and preheat the Big Green Egg to 250°F (121°C), using the convEGGtor for indirect grilling.

In a small bowl, mix together all of the ingredients for the dry rub. Cover the pork cubes with the mustard. Season them with the dry rub mixture, coating the pieces well. Let the pork cubes sit at room temperature while your Big Green Egg comes up to temp.

Once the Big Green Egg is ready, place the pork belly on a wire baking rack, place the baking rack inside the Big Green Egg and let the meat cook undisturbed for 1½ hours.

(continued)

Pork Belly Burnt Ends with Bourbon BBQ Sauce (continued)

BOURBON BBQ SAUCE

1 tbsp (15 ml) olive oil

1 cup (160 g) diced onion

3 cloves garlic

¾ cup (180 ml) bourbon

2 tbsp (30 ml) apple cider vinegar

1 tbsp (15 ml) Worcestershire sauce

1 tbsp (16 g) tomato paste

1 tsp dry mustard

¼ tsp cayenne

⅓ cup (73 g) brown sugar

2 cups (480 ml) ketchup

Kosher salt, to taste

Ground black pepper, to taste

While the pork is smoking, it is time to make your bourbon BBQ sauce. Heat the olive oil in a medium saucepan over medium heat. Add the onion and sauté it for 2 minutes, until it is soft. Add the garlic and sauté the mixture for 1 to 2 minutes, until the garlic is fragrant. Add the remaining ingredients for the sauce and bring the mixture to a low boil. Reduce the heat to low, then use an immersion blender to blend the mixture into a smooth sauce. Alternatively, carefully transfer the mixture to a countertop blender and blend it until a smooth sauce is formed, then pour the sauce back into the saucepan. Simmer the sauce for 30 minutes, until the sauce has thickened. Set the sauce aside and keep it warm.

At the 1½-hour mark, check the internal temperature of the pork belly cubes. When the internal temp measures 190°F (88°C), it is time to pull the pork belly cubes from the Big Green Egg. Place them in a half-sized aluminum pan and top them with the brown sugar and honey. Nestle the pieces of butter among the pork cubes. Cover the pan with aluminum foil and put the pan back in the smoker. Cook the pork for 60 to 90 minutes, until it is tender.

When the smoky pork cubes are tender, remove the foil from the pan, pour out the liquid from the pan and add the bourbon BBQ sauce. Carefully mix the sauce with the cubed pork, making sure each piece is covered with the sauce. Place the tray of sauced porky goodness back in the Big Green Egg so that the sauce can set. This should take no more than 10 minutes.

Pull the pan of pork belly off the Big Green Egg and transfer the sauced pork belly to a serving bowl.

FEEDS: 2–4 people

APPROXIMATE COOK TIME:
4–5 hours

BIG GREEN EGG SETUP:
Indirect

SUGGESTED WOOD TYPE:
Hickory or apple chunks

TOOLS AND ACCESSORIES:
convEGGtor

Saint Louis–Style Spareribs with Honey–Chipotle Glaze

People often ask me what my favorite thing to cook on a Big Green Egg is, and I find myself answering ribs every time. When ribs are done just right, you get the best of what BBQ has to offer: smoky flavor, tender meat and a sauce that balances both worlds. In this recipe, I do not use the Texas crutch (i.e., wrapping the ribs), as I find it produces a softer texture than I like with my ribs. The result of this recipe is perfectly smoked spareribs with a sauce that has just enough spice to balance everything else.

SMOKED SPARERIBS

1 rack spareribs

1 tbsp (15 ml) yellow mustard

PORK BBQ RUB

¼ cup (55 g) brown sugar

¼ cup (72 g) kosher salt

¼ cup (24 g) ground black pepper (ideally 16 mesh)

¼ cup (28 g) paprika

1 tbsp (9 g) garlic powder

1 tbsp (9 g) onion powder

Load the Big Green Egg with natural lump charcoal and mix in three chunks of hickory or apple wood with the lump charcoal (as described on page 16). Now light the charcoal and preheat the Big Green Egg to 250°F (121°C), using the convEGGtor for indirect grilling.

Trim the spareribs by removing the large section of bones on top of the ribs, which can be used for my BBQ Rib Tips (page 79). Next, flip the ribs over and remove the skirt. The skirt is the thin strip of meat that runs along the membrane on the bone side of the ribs. (Note that if you do not remove that extra meat, the ribs will be thicker at that section and take longer to cook.) You can easily remove the skirt by running a knife along the thin strip of meat above the membrane until it's completely cut off. Next, place a butter knife underneath the membrane of the third rib on the rack and pull up slightly. When the membrane separates from the bones, use a paper towel to grab the membrane and pull it off. Doing this will help ensure that the ribs are evenly seasoned and have a better mouthfeel when they are done. Finally, square up the ribs by removing the uneven ribs on both sides of your rack of spareribs until the shape of your spareribs resembles a rectangle.

In a small bowl, mix together all of the ingredients for the pork BBQ rub. Rub the mustard all over the trimmed rack of spareribs and cover the top, bottom and sides of the ribs with 4 teaspoons (16 g) of your pork BBQ rub. (Extra rub can be stored in an airtight container for 2 weeks.) Let the ribs sit at room temperature until your Big Green Egg is stable at 250°F (121°C) and the smoke is light gray in color. Place the ribs in your Big Green Egg bone side down and let them smoke undisturbed for 3 hours.

(continued)

Saint Louis–Style Spareribs with Honey–Chipotle Glaze (continued)

HONEY-CHIPOTLE GLAZE

2 tsp (10 ml) olive oil

½ yellow onion, diced

2 cloves garlic, minced

1½ cups (360 ml) ketchup

1 (12-oz [336-g]) can chipotle peppers in adobo sauce, peppers diced and sauce reserved

⅓ cup (80 ml) honey

⅛ cup (28 g) brown sugar

2 tbsp (30 ml) apple cider vinegar

1 tbsp (15 ml) Worcestershire sauce

1 tsp kosher salt

1 tsp ground black pepper

1 tsp paprika

SPRITZ (IF NEEDED)

1 cup (240 ml) apple juice

1 cup (240 ml) apple cider vinegar

While the ribs are smoking, make your honey-chipotle glaze. Heat the olive oil in a medium saucepan over medium heat. Add the onion and sauté it for 2 to 3 minutes. Next, add the garlic and cook the mixture for 1 to 2 minutes, until the garlic is fragrant. Add the remaining ingredients for the glaze and mix them together well. Reduce the heat to medium-low. Let the mixture simmer 10 to 15 minutes, stirring it often, until it has thickened. Use an immersion blender or countertop blender to blend the mixture to a silky consistency.

At the 3-hour mark, check on your ribs. If the bark looks dry, combine the apple juice and apple cider vinegar in a spray bottle and spritz the outside of the ribs. (You will likely have spritz left over after this cook; extra can be stored in the fridge for 2 weeks.) Close the lid to your Big Green Egg and smoke the ribs for 1 hour before checking on them again.

When checking the ribs an hour later—at this point, the ribs will have cooked for 4 hours total—you should see the bones sticking out ¾ inch (2 cm) and the internal temperature of the ribs should be close to 200°F (93°C). Brush the honey-chipotle glaze all over the meaty side of the ribs, reserving some of the glaze to serve, and let the ribs cook for another 10 to 15 minutes to set the glaze.

Remove the ribs from the Big Green Egg and let them rest for 15 to 20 minutes before slicing them and serving them with the reserved glaze.

FEEDS: 8–10 people

APPROXIMATE COOK TIME:
1–3 hours

BIG GREEN EGG SETUP:
Indirect

SUGGESTED WOOD TYPE:
Hickory or pecan chunks

TOOLS AND ACCESSORIES:
Butcher's twine,
convEGGtor, V-shaped
rack and roasting pan

BEEF

1 (6-lb [2.7-kg]) top or bottom round beef roast

2 tbsp (36 g) kosher salt

1 tbsp (15 ml) olive oil

10 kaiser rolls

1 Vidalia onion, thinly sliced

BEEF RUB

1 tbsp (6 g) ground black pepper (ideally 16 mesh)

1 tsp dried oregano

1 tsp garlic powder

1 tsp onion powder

1 tsp paprika

1 tsp chili powder

TIGER SAUCE

3 tbsp (45 g) prepared horseradish

½ cup (120 ml) mayonnaise

1 tsp fresh lemon juice

1 tsp minced garlic

Kosher salt, to taste

Ground black pepper, to taste

Baltimore–Style Pit Beef

I grew up in the Washington, DC, area and would often travel to see the Baltimore Orioles play baseball at the old Memorial Stadium. When my dad took me to games, he would always stop at Baker's Pit Beef and Tavern for one of their famous pit beef sandwiches. For this recipe, I re-created one of my favorite childhood food memories on the Big Green Egg.

The day before you cook the beef round roast, trim the excess fat and any silver skin from the roast. Tie the roast with butcher's twine to make it uniform in size; doing this will help with cooking time and the final shape of the roast for slicing. Now cover the entire roast with the kosher salt. Place the roast on a wire rack that is sitting in a baking pan and place the pan in the refrigerator overnight to dry-brine the roast.

The next day, load the Big Green Egg with natural lump charcoal and mix in three chunks of hickory or pecan wood with the lump charcoal (as described on page 16). Now light the charcoal and preheat the Big Green Egg to 225°F (107°C), using the convEGGtor for indirect grilling.

In a small bowl, mix together all of the ingredients for the beef rub. Remove the beef roast from the refrigerator, rub it with the olive oil and generously apply the beef rub to all sides of the roast. Let the seasoned beef roast sit at room temperature until the Big Green Egg comes up to temperature and the smoke is light gray in color. Place a V-shaped rack in a roasting pan, then place the roast on the rack. Place the roast in the Big Green Egg and let it smoke for 45 minutes. At the 45-minute mark, check your roast and flip it over to the other side, so that all sides brown evenly. Smoke the roast for about 45 minutes, until its internal temperature measures 110°F (43°C).

While the beef is smoking, make the tiger sauce by mixing together all of the ingredients for the sauce in a medium bowl. Set the bowl of tiger sauce in the refrigerator until you are ready to serve the beef.

When the internal temperature of the roast hits 110°F (43°C), remove the roast and increase the heat in your Big Green Egg to 450°F (232°C). When the temperature has been reached and is stable, place the roast back inside the Big Green Egg for 10 to 15 minutes, until it is nicely browned all over. Remove the roast and let it rest for 30 minutes.

After the roast has rested, find the grain and start slicing thinly against the grain. The thinner the slices, the better. Once you get the beef sliced, assemble your sandwiches by slathering some of the tiger sauce on a kaiser roll, piling the meat on and topping the meat with some of the thinly sliced onion.

FEEDS: 10–12 people

APPROXIMATE COOK TIME:
3–4 hours

BIG GREEN EGG SETUP:
Indirect

SUGGESTED WOOD TYPE:
Apple or cherry chunks

TOOLS AND ACCESSORIES:
convEGGtor, roasting pan
and V-shaped rack

HAM

1 bone-in ham (I used a
kurobuta ham from Snake
River Farms®)

1 tbsp (15 ml) yellow mustard

3 tbsp (36 g) BBQ rub of your
choice

3 cups (720 ml) apple juice

1 yellow onion, cut into
¼" (6-mm) pieces

GLAZE

½ cup (110 g) brown sugar

½ cup (120 ml) pineapple
juice

½ cup (120 ml) mirin

¼ cup (72 g) gochujang paste

3 cloves garlic, minced

1" (2.5-cm) piece fresh ginger,
grated

1 tbsp (15 ml) toasted
sesame oil

1 tbsp (15 ml) soy sauce

1 tbsp (15 ml) fresh lime juice

Kurobuta Bone–In Ham with Gochujang Glaze

There is nothing like a beautifully glazed ham adorning the dinner table during the holidays. For this recipe, I use a kurobuta ham; the word kurobuta translates to "black pig" in Japanese. This variety of pork comes from the Japanese program for purebred Berkshire pigs. Their breeding produces maximum marbling, which in turn produces amazing flavor. For this rich ham, I came up with a sweet and spicy glaze to balance the flavors perfectly.

Load the Big Green Egg with natural lump charcoal and mix in three chunks of apple or cherry wood with the lump charcoal (as described on page 16). Now light the charcoal and preheat the Big Green Egg to 250°F (121°C), using the convEGGtor for indirect grilling.

Take the ham out of the packaging and dry it off with a paper towel. Score the outside of the ham to help the rub work its way into the meat. Slather the ham with the mustard and apply the BBQ rub all over the ham.

In the roasting pan, combine the apple juice and onion. Put the ham on a V-shaped rack, then place the rack in the roasting pan.

When the Big Green Egg is steady at 250°F (121°C) and the smoke is light gray in color, place the roasting rack on the grill grate. Close the lid and smoke the ham undisturbed for 2 hours.

At the 2-hour mark, cover the roasting pan and the ham with aluminum foil. Cook the ham for 1 hour.

While the ham continues to cook, make your glaze. Combine all of the ingredients for the glaze in a medium saucepan, mixing them well. Bring the mixture to a low boil over high heat. Reduce the heat to medium-low and let the glaze simmer for about 30 minutes, until it thickens.

After the ham has cooked for 3 hours, gently uncover the ham and apply the glaze all over it, reserving some of the glaze for serving. Cook the ham uncovered for 30 minutes, until the internal temperature of the ham reaches 140°F (60°C). Remove the ham from the Big Green Egg, let it rest for 30 minutes and then slice it and serve it with the reserved glaze.

FEEDS: 6–8 people

APPROXIMATE COOK TIME:
5–8 hours

BIG GREEN EGG SETUP:
Indirect

SUGGESTED WOOD TYPE:
Hickory or cherry chunks

TOOLS AND ACCESSORIES:
convEGGtor, pink butcher
paper

4 lb (1.8 kg) corned beef

¼ cup (24 g) ground coriander

3 tbsp (18 g) ground black
pepper (ideally 16 mesh)

2 tsp (6 g) garlic powder

2 tbsp (14 g) paprika

Smoked Pastrami

A hot pastrami on rye is one of my favorite sandwiches. So, when it gets closer to Saint Patrick's Day, there is ample opportunity to find corned beef and turn that into delicious pastrami by smoking it on the Big Green Egg. For this recipe, I use an American Wagyu corned beef brisket from Snake River Farms. However, any corned beef you find at the grocery store will work perfectly for this.

The night before you plan to smoke your corned beef, put the corned beef in a container larger than the meat and cover it with cold water. Place the container in the fridge for at least 8 hours to desalinate the corned beef. To remove as much salt as possible, you will want to change the water at least once.

The next day, make the dry rub by mixing together the coriander, pepper, garlic powder and paprika in a small bowl. Rinse the meat and apply 3 tablespoons (36 g) of the rub while the meat is still wet (the extra rub can be stored in an airtight container for 2 weeks). Note that there is no salt in this rub recipe, since the corned beef still has plenty inside—adding more would make it too salty.

Load the Big Green Egg with natural lump charcoal and mix in three chunks of hickory or cherry wood with the lump charcoal (as described on page 16). Now light the charcoal and preheat the Big Green Egg to 225°F (107°C), using the convEGGtor for indirect grilling.

When the Big Green Egg is holding steady at your desired temperature and the smoke is light gray in color, place the meat inside. Smoke the corned beef until it reaches 165°F (74°C) internally and the crust is mahogany in color. Next, wrap it in pink butcher paper and place it back in the Big Green Egg. Smoke the wrapped corned beef until it reaches an internal temperature of 204°F (96°C).

Remove the wrapped smoked corned beef, which is now pastrami, from your Big Green Egg. Allow the pastrami to rest for 1 hour before slicing it thinly against the grain for tender and juicy slices of homemade pastrami.

TOOLS AND ACCESSORIES:
convEGGtor, full-sized
aluminum steam table pan

LEG OF LAMB

5–7-lb (2.3–3.2-kg) leg of lamb

2 tbsp (30 ml) olive oil

3 tbsp (36 g) your favorite
BBQ beef rub (I used Dizzy
Pig Cow Lick Spicy Beef Rub)
or a 50/50 mix kosher salt and
coarsely ground black pepper)

GARLIC AND ROSEMARY JUS

2 cups (480 ml) beef stock

½ yellow onion, diced

2 carrots, diced

2 ribs celery, diced

10 cloves garlic, minced

3 sprigs fresh rosemary

Smoked Leg of Lamb with Garlic and Rosemary Jus

If there is one go-to meal at my house to celebrate Easter, it is smoked leg of lamb. The slow-smoked lamb is a beautiful and tasty centerpiece to my table. Paired with an amazing jus, this lamb recipe really shines. Treat lamb as you would beef when thinking about the finishing temperature. For this recipe, I smoked the lamb to a perfect medium-rare, which is juicy and flavorful.

Load the Big Green Egg with natural lump charcoal and mix in three chunks of pecan or oak wood with the lump charcoal (as described on page 16). Now light the charcoal and preheat the Big Green Egg to 250°F (121°C), using the convEGGtor for indirect grilling.

Rub the lamb with the olive oil and then season it all over with the BBQ beef rub. Let the lamb rest at room temperature while your Big Green Egg comes up to temperature.

In a full-sized aluminum steam table pan, combine all of the ingredients for the garlic and rosemary jus. Place the steam table pan underneath the spot you intend to put the leg of lamb in order to catch all the drippings while the leg of lamb smokes. Place the seasoned lamb on the grill grate directly above the drip pan. Let the lamb smoke for 1 hour undisturbed before checking its internal temperature.

Once the leg of lamb reaches an internal temp of 120°F (49°C; this usually takes about 2 hours), remove the leg of lamb and the pan containing the garlic and rosemary jus. Close the lid of your Big Green Egg and bring the temperature up to 350°F (177°C).

While you wait for the Big Green Egg's temperature to rise, strain the jus and set it aside, keeping it warm until your lamb is ready to serve. Once the Big Green Egg's temperature is stable at 350°F (177°C), place the leg of lamb back inside and roast it for 20 to 30 minutes, until the meat's internal temperature is 135°F (57°C) and its color is dark brown. Remove the lamb from the Big Green Egg and let it rest for 10 minutes.

Once the Lamb has rested, it is time to slice it and serve it with that delicious garlic and rosemary jus.

FEEDS: 2–4 people

APPROXIMATE COOK TIME:
3–4 hours

BIG GREEN EGG SETUP:
Indirect

SUGGESTED WOOD TYPE:
Hickory or apple chunks

TOOLS AND ACCESSORIES:
convEGGtor

BABY BACK RIBS

1 rack baby back ribs

1 tbsp (18 g) kosher salt

1 tbsp (6 g) ground black
pepper (ideally 16 mesh)

1 tbsp (7 g) paprika

1 tsp yellow mustard

2 tbsp (28 g) unsalted butter,
sliced into 4 equal portions

¼ cup (55 g) brown sugar

½ cup (120 ml) apple juice

1 cup (240 ml) your favorite
BBQ sauce

SPRITZ

1 cup (240 ml) apple cider
vinegar

1 cup (240 ml) apple juice

Baby Back Ribs Hot and Fast

Sometimes you want to eat smoky and delicious ribs sooner than it typically takes to smoke them low and slow. This recipe bumps the temperature up high enough to cook the ribs in less time but without sacrificing flavor or texture. The secret is using the Texas crutch: wrapping the ribs in foil to help speed up the cooking time. For this recipe, you can use any of the BBQ sauce recipes used throughout this book or your favorite off-the-shelf brand.

Load the Big Green Egg with natural lump charcoal and mix in three chunks of hickory or apple wood with in the lump charcoal (as described on page 16). Now light the charcoal and preheat the Big Green Egg to 300°F (149°C), using the convEGGtor for indirect grilling.

To prepare the baby back ribs, trim the ribs of the skirt, excess fat and membrane. In a small bowl, mix together the salt, pepper and paprika for the dry rub. Slather the mustard over the ribs, and then season the ribs with the dry rub. Let the ribs sit at room temperature while your Big Green Egg is preheating.

When the Big Green Egg is stable at 300°F (149°C) and the smoke is light gray, place the ribs inside bone side down. Smoke the ribs undisturbed for 1 hour. During this time, make the spritz by mixing together the apple cider vinegar and apple juice in a spray bottle. (You will likely have spritz left over after this cook; extra can be stored in the fridge for 2 weeks.) At the 1-hour mark, start spritzing your ribs every 30 minutes.

After the ribs have cooked for 2 hours total, place two sheets of heavy-duty aluminum foil on the counter. Top the foil with the butter and brown sugar. Next, remove the ribs from the Big Green Egg and place the ribs meat side down on the butter and brown sugar. Fold the foil up around the ribs to create a "boat," then pour in the apple juice. Seal the foil around the ribs tightly and place them back in the Big Green Egg to cook for 1 hour.

After the ribs have cooked for 1 hour in the foil—for a total cooking time of 3 hours—carefully remove the ribs from the foil, watching for steam, and brush them with the BBQ sauce. Place the ribs back in the Big Green Egg for 10 to 15 minutes to set the sauce. Remove the ribs and let them rest for 15 minutes before slicing them.

FEEDS: 6–8 people

APPROXIMATE COOK TIME:
5–7 hours

BIG GREEN EGG SETUP:
Indirect

SUGGESTED WOOD TYPE:
Hickory or oak chunks

TOOLS AND ACCESSORIES:
Butcher's twine,
convEGGtor

8–10-lb (3.6–4.5-kg) boneless prime rib roast

1 tsp kosher salt per pound of rib roast

2 sticks unsalted butter, softened

5 cloves garlic, minced

1 tbsp (2 g) minced fresh rosemary

1 tbsp (2 g) minced fresh thyme

2 tbsp (24 g) your favorite BBQ dry rub (I used Dizzy Pig Cow Lick Spicy Beef Rub)

Smoked Boneless Prime Rib Roast

Prime rib is my favorite meal to cook during the holidays. Nothing sets the mood better than a perfectly smoked prime rib roast as the centerpiece of your table. Smoking this large cut of beef low and slow produces amazing flavor and a beautiful exterior. It can be smoked, wrapped and held in a cooler well ahead of your guests' arrival, allowing you to simply enjoy the holiday cheer.

The day before you plan to smoke your prime rib, take the meat out of the packaging and season the prime rib roast by sprinkling the kosher salt all over the meat. Use butcher's twine to tie up the roast in at least four spots to hold the meat in place while it slowly cooks. Place a wire rack on a baking sheet, and then place the seasoned and tied roast on the wire rack so all sides of the meat are exposed to the air. Refrigerate the roast, uncovered and still on the baking sheet, overnight.

The next day, take the roast out of the refrigerator 1 hour before you place it on the Big Green Egg. Load the Big Green Egg with natural lump charcoal and mix in three chunks of hickory or oak wood with the lump charcoal (as described on page 16). Now light the charcoal and preheat the Big Green Egg to 225°F (107°C), using the convEGGtor for indirect grilling.

In a medium bowl, combine the butter, garlic, rosemary, thyme and dry rub. Apply the butter mixture all over the exposed meat of the roast.

When the Big Green Egg's temperature is stable at 225°F (107°C) and the smoke is light gray in color, place the prime rib roast inside the Big Green Egg and let it smoke undisturbed until the center of the roast measures 125°F (52°C) on an instant-read thermometer. At this temperature, you can estimate a cooking time of 40 minutes per pound of meat, so it will likely take 5 to 7 hours to reach the desired internal temperature.

Remove the prime rib roast from the Big Green Egg, tent it loosely with foil and let it rest for at least 30 minutes before slicing it.

FEEDS: 6–8 people

APPROXIMATE COOK TIME:
5–6 hours

BIG GREEN EGG SETUP:
Indirect

SUGGESTED WOOD TYPE:
Hickory or cherry chunks

TOOLS AND ACCESSORIES:
convEGGtor, full-sized
aluminum pan

COUNTRY-STYLE RIBS

3 lb (1.4 kg) country-style
pork ribs

2 tbsp (30 ml) yellow mustard

1 yellow onion, thinly sliced

2 carrots, diced

2 ribs celery, diced

4 cloves garlic, smashed

2 cups (480 ml) chicken stock

½ cup (120 ml) apple juice

1 cup (240 ml) BBQ sauce

PORK BBQ RUB

¼ cup (55 g) brown sugar

¼ cup (72 g) kosher salt

¼ cup (24 g) ground black
pepper (ideally 16 mesh)

¼ cup (28 g) paprika

1 tbsp (9 g) garlic powder

1 tbsp (9 g) onion powder

Smoked Country–Style Ribs

Smoked country-style ribs are not ribs at all! In fact, this cut comes from the shoulder of the pig, which is the same section that contains the larger cut used for smoked pork shoulder. This tasty smoked meat is a great way to produce a comforting dinner for friends and family in less time than it would take to smoke whole pork shoulder. Meaty, smoky and packed with flavor, these country-style ribs will not disappoint.

Load the Big Green Egg with natural lump charcoal and mix in three chunks of hickory or cherry wood with the lump charcoal (as described on page 16). Now light the charcoal and preheat the Big Green Egg to 250°F (121°C), using the convEGGtor for indirect grilling.

Remove the country-style ribs from the packaging and trim off any excess fat, leftover pieces of bone and silver skin. In a small bowl, mix together all of the ingredients for the pork BBQ rub. Pour the yellow mustard over the country-style ribs and spread it across the meat evenly—the mustard will act as a binder for your rub. Next, cover the country-style ribs with about 2 tablespoons (24 g) of the pork BBQ rub. (Extra rub can be stored in an airtight container for 2 weeks.) Let the ribs sit until your Big Green Egg has stabilized at 250°F (121°C) and the smoke is light gray in color.

When the Big Green Egg is ready, place the seasoned country-style ribs inside and close the lid. Leave the country-style ribs alone for the first 3 hours of the smoke, and then check their temperature. You are looking for the bark to be a rich, dark color and the internal temperature of the meat to be 165°F (74°C) before moving to the next step. If the ribs need more time—either because the bark hasn't set or the internal temperature is too low—close the lid of the Big Green Egg and let them smoke for 1 hour before checking the temperature again.

When the country-style ribs are ready, remove them from the Big Green Egg and place them in a full-sized aluminum pan along with the onion, carrots, celery, garlic, chicken stock and apple juice. Pour the BBQ sauce over the country-style ribs and cover the pan tightly with foil. Place the pan in your Big Green Egg and cook the country-style ribs for 2 hours before checking to see if they are done. You will know the ribs are ready when their internal temperature is between 200 and 204°F (93 and 96°C), they are fork-tender and they shred easily. If the ribs are not done yet, cover the pan again and place the pan back in the Big Green Egg for 1 hour before checking the meat again.

When the country-style ribs are completely cooked, remove the ribs from the pan and allow them to rest 30 minutes before serving them. If you like, you can strain the braising liquid and reserve it for an easy sauce to pour over your country-style ribs when serving them.

Smoked Lobster Tails

Smoked lobster tails are one of my most favorite treats to serve guests. Tasting the little kiss of smoke inside every bite of the sweet lobster meat is quite an experience. The trick to this recipe is watching the internal temperature of the meat, so that you don't go past 140°F (60°C) while the lobster tails are smoking. When you catch the smoked lobster at the right point, a tasty treat awaits you! My favorite place to get great lobster tails is online at LobsterAnywhere.com.

FEEDS: 2–4 people

APPROXIMATE COOK TIME:
1–1½ hours

BIG GREEN EGG SETUP:
Indirect

SUGGESTED WOOD TYPE:
Alder or apple chunks

TOOLS AND ACCESSORIES:
convEGGtor, small cast-iron saucepan

4 (6-oz [168-g]) lobster tails

2 tsp (8 g) your favorite BBQ rub (I used Dizzy Pig Shakin' the Tree Lemon Pepper Seasoning)

1 stick salted butter, cubed

Lemon wedges

Finely chopped fresh parsley

Load the Big Green Egg with natural lump charcoal and mix in two chunks of alder or apple wood with the lump charcoal (as described on page 16). Now light the charcoal and preheat the Big Green Egg to 225°F (107°C), using the convEGGtor for indirect grilling.

Take the lobster tails out of the packaging and drain any excess liquid. Use kitchen shears to cut down the middle of each shell, all the way to the tip of the tail. Gently spread the shell apart and begin to pull the meat out, leaving the tip of the meat attached at the end of the tail, and gently rest it on top of the split shell. Season the exposed lobster meat with your BBQ rub.

Place the lobster tails in the Big Green Egg shell side down. Let the tails smoke for 30 minutes. At this point, place the butter in a small cast-iron saucepan and put the saucepan in the Big Green Egg to allow the butter to melt and take on a hint of smoke flavor while the lobster finishes cooking.

After 30 minutes, check the internal temperature of the lobster tails: Once they measure 110°F (43°C), start basting the tails with the smoked butter every 10 minutes.

In another 45 to 60 minutes, your lobster tails should measure 140°F (60°C) internally; when they reach this point, remove the lobster tails and butter. You can remove the meat from the shells or you can serve the lobster meat sitting on top of the shells for a beautiful presentation. Garnish the lobster with the lemon wedges and parsley.

FEEDS: 4 people

APPROXIMATE COOK TIME:
2–3 hours

BIG GREEN EGG SETUP:
Indirect

SUGGESTED WOOD TYPE:
Hickory or oak chunks

TOOLS AND ACCESSORIES:
convEGGtor, wire baking rack

1 whole chicken

2 tsp (4 g) paprika

1 tsp (3 g) garlic powder

1 tsp (3 g) onion powder

1 tbsp (14 g) brown sugar

2 tsp (4 g) ground black pepper (ideally 16 mesh)

1 tsp ground cumin

2 tsp (12 g) kosher salt

1 tbsp (15 ml) olive oil

Texas–Style Chicken Halves

One of my favorite BBQ chefs is Aaron Franklin of Franklin Barbecue in Austin, Texas. He is best known for his brisket, but he has produced some other amazing smoked meats, including chicken. This recipe is heavily influenced by Aaron and his style of BBQ. Smoky, moist and delicious, this smoked chicken dish is a keeper!

Load the Big Green Egg with natural lump charcoal and mix in three chunks of hickory or oak wood with the lump charcoal (as described on page 16). Now light the charcoal and preheat the Big Green Egg to 250°F (121°C), using the convEGGtor for indirect grilling.

Remove the chicken from the packaging and use paper towels to pat the whole chicken dry, removing any excess giblets and debris from inside of the chicken. Cut the backbone out of the chicken using a sharp knife or kitchen shears. Clean up and remove any of the ribs still in place. To flatten the bird, place the chicken breast side up, then press down hard with your hands until you hear that breastplate pop. With the bird still facing you breast side up, cut the breastbone right down the middle of the chicken breast, until you have two separate chicken halves. Trim the chicken halves of any extra skin.

In a small bowl, mix together the paprika, garlic powder, onion powder, brown sugar, pepper, cumin and salt. Add the olive oil, mixing the ingredients until they are well combined. Rub the mixture over the chicken halves, covering both the front and back. Place the chicken halves breast side up on a wire baking rack. This will help you move the chicken in and out of the Big Green Egg without disturbing the chicken skin as it cooks. Let the chicken sit on the wire rack at room temperature until your Big Green Egg stabilizes at 250°F (121°C) and the smoke is light gray in color.

When the Big Green Egg is ready, place the wire rack with the chicken halves on the Big Green Egg and close the lid. Let the chicken smoke for 2 hours at 250°F (121°C), then increase the temperature to 450°F (232°C) and smoke the chicken for 30 minutes to crisp the skin. The chicken is ready when its internal temperature measures at least 160°F (71°C) in the thickest part of the breast (the internal temp will continue to rise while the meat rests).

Take the chicken off the Big Green Egg and let it rest for 20 to 30 minutes before carving it.

FEEDS: 4 people

APPROXIMATE COOK TIME:
2–3 hours

BIG GREEN EGG SETUP:
Indirect

SUGGESTED WOOD TYPE:
Hickory or oak chunks

TOOLS AND ACCESSORIES:
convEGGtor

CHICKEN WINGS

2 lb (908 g) chicken wings

1 tbsp (15 ml) olive oil

4 tbsp (48 g) your favorite
Cajun seasoning, divided
(I used Dizzy Pig Bayou-ish™
Blackening Seasoning)

MERMAN BBQ SAUCE

1 cup (240 ml) yellow mustard

¼ cup (60 ml) honey

¼ cup (60 ml) apple cider
vinegar

2 tbsp (30 ml) ketchup

2 tbsp (28 g) brown sugar

1 tbsp (15 ml) Worcestershire
sauce

1 tsp garlic powder

1 tsp onion powder

¼ tsp chipotle chili powder

½ tsp ground black pepper
(ideally 16 mesh)

1 tsp salt

1 tsp hot sauce

"Merman" Chicken Wings

Since moving to Gulfport, Florida, I have been on the lookout for the best BBQ restaurants near me. One of my favorite places for BBQ, oddly enough, is a seafood restaurant called Mullet's Fish Camp and Market. They have an 80-gallon (303-L) reverse-flow smoker on-site where they smoke their fish and their wings. The wings are some of the tastiest I have had. This is my version of their signature dish, Merman Wings.

Load the Big Green Egg with natural lump charcoal and mix in two chunks of hickory or oak wood with the lump charcoal (as described on page 16). Now light the charcoal and preheat the Big Green Egg to 250°F (121°C), using the convEGGtor for indirect grilling.

If you bought whole chicken wings, separate the drums from the flats and discard the tips. Place the wing parts in a large bowl, then toss them with the olive oil. Toss the wings with 2 tablespoons (24 g) of the Cajun seasoning, ensuring that the wings are coated.

Once the Big Green Egg is stable at 250°F (121°C) and the smoke is light gray in color, place the wings in the Big Green Egg and cook them for 1 hour. At the 1-hour mark, flip the wings and smoke them for 1 hour on the other side.

While the wings are smoking, heat a small skillet over medium heat. Add the remaining 2 tablespoons (24 g) of the Cajun seasoning and cook it for 3 to 4 minutes, until the seasoning smokes and is nicely charred. Set the Cajun seasoning aside.

Next, make the Merman BBQ sauce by mixing together all of the sauce ingredients in a medium saucepan over medium heat. Cook the mixture until it reaches a low boil, the sugar has dissolved and the ingredients are evenly combined. Remove the sauce from the heat and mix in the charred Cajun seasoning.

At the 2-hour mark, increase the temperature of your Big Green Egg to 350°F (177°C) and cook the wings for another 25 to 30 minutes. At this point the chicken skin should be deep brown and crispy with a little char. Remove the wings and toss them with three-quarters of the Merman BBQ sauce. Serve the sauced wings with the remaining BBQ sauce for dipping.

FEEDS: 10–12 people

APPROXIMATE COOK TIME: 5–6 hours

BIG GREEN EGG SETUP: Indirect

SUGGESTED WOOD TYPE: Hickory or apple chunks

TOOLS AND ACCESSORIES: convEGGtor, meat syringe or meat injector, half-sized aluminum pan

PORK

1 (8-lb [3.6-kg]) pork butt or pork shoulder

2 tbsp (30 ml) yellow mustard

1 cup (240 ml) apple juice

PORK INJECTION FLUID

¾ cup (180 ml) apple juice

½ cup (120 ml) water

¼ cup (60 ml) apple cider vinegar

¼ cup (72 g) kosher salt

¼ cup (50 g) sugar

2 tbsp (30 ml) Worcestershire sauce

DRY RUB

¼ cup (55 g) brown sugar

¼ cup (28 g) paprika

3 tbsp (54 g) kosher salt

2 tbsp (12 g) ground black pepper

2 tbsp (12 g) ground cumin

2 tbsp (18 g) chili powder

1 tbsp (6 g) cayenne

2 tsp (4 g) dry mustard

Hot and Fast Pulled Pork (a.k.a. Turbo Butt)

If you want to get a smoky and delicious pulled pork sandwich in half the time it would take using a traditional recipe, then you have come to the right place. This recipe takes advantage of injecting the meat to help season it and keep it moist while it smokes at a much higher temperature than its traditional low and slow counterpart. You will be surprised at how good this hot and fast pulled pork turns out.

Load the Big Green Egg with natural lump charcoal and mix in four chunks of hickory or apple wood with the lump charcoal (as described on page 16). Now light the charcoal and preheat the Big Green Egg to 350°F (177°C), using the convEGGtor for indirect grilling.

Remove the pork butt from the package and place it on a cutting board. In a large measuring cup, mix together all of the ingredients for the pork injection fluid. Use a meat syringe or meat injector to inject your pork shoulder with the injection fluid. When you inject the fluid, make sure you do so in several different spots all over the pork shoulder to ensure better flavor throughout the meat.

Next, in a medium bowl, mix together all of the ingredients for the dry rub. Cut the pork's fat cap in a crosshatch pattern ¼ inch (6 mm) deep, and then cover the whole pork shoulder with the yellow mustard to create a binder for the rub. Apply 3 tablespoons (36 g) of the dry rub to the pork and work it into the meat, including the creases created by the crosshatch cuts on the fat cap.

Once the Big Green Egg is up to temperature and the smoke is light gray in color, place the pork shoulder in, fat cap down, and let it smoke undisturbed for 3 hours.

At the 3-hour mark, remove the pork shoulder and place it in a half-sized aluminum pan. Add the apple juice to the bottom of the pan, cover the pan with aluminum foil and place it in the Big Green Egg. Let the pork cook for 2 hours, until its internal temperature reaches 195°F (91°C).

Remove the pork shoulder from the Big Green Egg and crack the seal in the covered aluminum pan, allowing some of the steam to escape. Let the pork rest for 1 hour before pulling the pork.

FEEDS: 4–6 people

APPROXIMATE COOK TIME:
2–3 hours

BIG GREEN EGG SETUP:
Indirect

SUGGESTED WOOD TYPE:
Pecan or apple chunks

TOOLS AND ACCESSORIES:
convEGGtor

PORK LOIN

4–5-lb (1.8–2.3-kg) pork loin roast

1 tbsp (15 ml) yellow mustard

DRY RUB

¼ cup (55 g) brown sugar

¼ cup (72 g) kosher salt

¼ cup (24 g) ground black pepper (ideally 16 mesh)

¼ cup (28 g) paprika

1 tbsp (6 g) dry mustard

1 tbsp (9 g) granulated garlic

1 tsp cayenne

Smoked Pork Loin Roast

Pork loin is the perfect thing to smoke when you're feeding a large group of hungry people and you do not want to fuss with the cook while they wait. Pork loin is a very lean cut from the pig, so watching this meat is essential—otherwise, it will overcook. The combination of the smoke from the smoldering wood chunks and the dry rub gives this dish an amazing flavor.

Load the Big Green Egg with natural lump charcoal and mix in three chunks of pecan or apple wood with the lump charcoal (as described on page 16). Now light the charcoal and preheat the Big Green Egg to 225°F (107°C), using the convEGGtor for indirect grilling.

Remove the pork loin roast from the packaging and pat it dry with a paper towel. You will want to remove excess fat if the fat cap is more than ¼ inch (6 mm) thick. Next, using a sharp knife, cut a crosshatch pattern ¼ inch (6 mm) deep in the fat cap. Scoring the meat like this allows you to work the mustard binder and dry rub down into the meat. In a small bowl, mix together all of the ingredients for the dry rub. Rub the pork with the yellow mustard so there is a thin layer all over the outside of the pork loin roast. Now generously season the pork all over with about 3 tablespoons (36 g) of the dry rub. (Extra dry rub can be stored in an airtight container for 2 weeks.)

Once the Big Green Egg is stable at 225°F (107°C) and the smoke is light gray in color, place the seasoned pork loin roast inside and smoke the pork until its internal temperature is 145°F (63°C); this should take 2 to 3 hours.

When you reach the final internal temperature of 145°F (63°C), remove the pork loin roast from the Big Green Egg and let the meat rest for 20 minutes, loosely tented with foil. Slice the roast and serve it to your friends and family, who have been waiting patiently for this delicious smoked treat.

FEEDS: 4 people

APPROXIMATE COOK TIME:
6–8 hours

BIG GREEN EGG SETUP:
Indirect

SUGGESTED WOOD TYPE:
Hickory or oak chunks

TOOLS AND ACCESSORIES:
convEGGtor, pink butcher
paper

TRI-TIP

1 (2–3-lb [908-g to 1.4-kg])
tri-tip beef (I used Snake
River Farms American
Wagyu Black Grade Tri-Tip)

2 tbsp (30 ml) hot sauce

BRISKET SEASONING

¼ cup (24 g) ground black
pepper (ideally 16 mesh)

2 tbsp (10 g) Lawry's
Seasoned Salt

2 tbsp (36 g) kosher salt

"Brisket–Style" Tri-Tip

Tri-tip is a cut that has been popularized on the West Coast and is often referred to as the Santa Maria tri-tip roast. It is a well-marbled cut from the bottom of the loin section of a cow. With this recipe, I show you how to smoke this cut just like a brisket so you can get a delicious smoked piece of beef in far less time.

Load the Big Green Egg with natural lump charcoal and mix in two chunks of hickory or oak wood with the lump charcoal (as described on page 16). Now light the charcoal and preheat the Big Green Egg to 225°F (107°C), using the convEGGtor for indirect grilling.

Prepare your tri-tip by trimming any excess fat and the silver skin. In a small bowl, mix together all of the ingredients for the brisket seasoning. Rub the hot sauce all over your tri-tip to act as a binder for the seasoning. Next, generously season your tri-tip all over with 1 to 2 tablespoons (12 to 24 g) of the brisket seasoning. (Extra seasoning can be stored in an airtight container for 2 weeks.) Let the tri-tip rest at room temperature as your Big Green Egg comes up to temperature.

Once the Big Green Egg is stable at 225°F (107°C) and the smoke is light blue in color, place the tri-tip inside and smoke it until its internal temperature reaches 165°F (74°C); this usually takes about 5 hours. While the tri-tip is smoking, look for dry spots forming on the pellicle and spritz the tri-tip with water as necessary to ensure proper humidity in the smoking environment.

When the internal temperature of the tri-tip is 165°F (74°C) and the bark is deep mahogany in color, remove the tri-tip from the Big Green Egg and wrap it in pink butcher paper. Place the wrapped tri-tip back in the Big Green Egg and cook until the internal temperature reaches 204°F (96°C), which usually takes another 3 hours, and the meat is probe-tender.

Remove the tri-tip from the Big Green Egg and let it rest for 30 minutes, still wrapped in the butcher paper, before slicing it.

RIB TIPS

2 slab rib tips (about 4 lb [1.8 kg])

2 tbsp (30 ml) yellow mustard

¼ cup (60 ml) apple juice

½ cup (120 ml) your favorite BBQ sauce

PORK BBQ RUB

¼ cup (55 g) brown sugar

¼ cup (72 g) kosher salt

¼ cup (24 g) coarsely ground black pepper

¼ cup (28 g) paprika

1 tbsp (9 g) garlic powder

1 tbsp (9 g) onion powder

BBQ Rib Tips

One of my favorite things about cooking spareribs is using the trimmings for tasty treats. When I get a full rack of spareribs and trim them down to a Saint Louis cut, I am left with a whole section of rib tips. This recipe walks you through how to turn this trimmed section into a deliciously smoky treat.

Load the Big Green Egg with natural lump charcoal and mix in three chunks of hickory or pecan wood with the lump charcoal (as described on page 16). Now light the charcoal and preheat the Big Green Egg to 250°F (121°C), using the convEGGtor for indirect grilling.

Prepare the rib tips by cutting them into 4-inch (10-cm) sections. In a small bowl, mix together all of the ingredients for the pork BBQ rub. Slather the rib tips with the mustard to create a binder for the pork BBQ rub. Then use 4 tablespoons (48 g) of the pork BBQ rub to cover all sides of the rib tips. (Extra pork BBQ rub can be stored in an airtight container for 2 weeks.)

Once the Big Green Egg is stable at 250°F (121°C) and the smoke is light blue in color, place the seasoned rib tips inside and allow them to smoke undisturbed for 3 hours.

At the 3-hour mark, take the rib tips out of the Big Green Egg, place them in a half-sized aluminum pan, add the apple juice to the bottom of the pan and cover the pan with aluminum foil. Place the covered pan in the Big Green Egg and allow the rib tips to cook for 1 hour.

At the 1-hour mark, remove the rib tips from the pan, brush them with the BBQ sauce and place the pan back on the Big Green Egg to cook for 30 minutes, until the sauce is set and the internal temperature of the rib tips is 185°F (85°C). Remove the rib tips from the Big Green Egg and let them rest for 15 minutes before serving them.

FEEDS: 6–8 people

APPROXIMATE COOK TIME: 8–10 hours

BIG GREEN EGG SETUP: Indirect

SUGGESTED WOOD TYPE: Hickory or oak chunks

TOOLS AND ACCESSORIES: convEGGtor, ¼ steam table pan, half-sized aluminum pan

BRISKET

1 (5-lb [2.3-kg]) brisket flat

2 tbsp (30 ml) hot sauce (such as Cholula)

BEEF RUB

2 tbsp (36 g) kosher salt

2 tbsp (12 g) ground black pepper (ideally 16 mesh)

1 tbsp (9 g) garlic powder

1 tbsp (7 g) smoked paprika

SPRITZ

1 cup (240 ml) apple cider vinegar

1 cup (240 ml) water

¼–½ tsp Worcestershire sauce

¼–½ tsp hot sauce

Smoked Brisket Flat

When I first started smoking meats, the only brisket I could find was a brisket flat at my local grocery store. For those new to the BBQ world, like I was at the time, a whole brisket consists of two separate muscles: the point and the flat. Finding a whole packer brisket can be done, but typically not at your neighborhood grocery. So smoking a brisket flat was my entry point into learning about smoking brisket. The flat is a much easier cook to manage and in turn a better vehicle to learn with. Start small with this cook and master it before moving on to cooking a whole brisket with both muscles.

Load the Big Green Egg with natural lump charcoal and mix in three chunks of hickory or oak wood with the lump charcoal (as described on page 16). Now light the charcoal and preheat the Big Green Egg to 250°F (121°C), using the convEGGtor for indirect grilling.

Remove the brisket flat from the refrigerator and place it on a cutting board. In a small bowl, mix together all of the ingredients for the beef rub. Slather the hot sauce over all sides of the brisket flat and season the meat on all sides with the beef rub. Let the seasoned brisket flat sit at room temperature while your Big Green Egg continues to preheat.

Once the Big Green Egg is stable at 250°F (121°C) and the smoke is light gray in color, place the brisket flat inside and allow it to smoke for 3 hours before checking it. I like to put a ¼ steam table pan filled with warm water in with the brisket flat while it smokes to help manage the humidity.

In a spray bottle, mix together all of the ingredients for the spritz. After the brisket flat has been 3 hours in the smoke, start spritzing it every 45 to 60 minutes. Continue smoking until the brisket flat has reached an internal temperature of 165°F (74°C). At this point, place the brisket flat in a half-sized aluminum pan, spritz the flat one last time and cover the pan with foil. Place the covered pan in the Big Green Egg and continue cooking the meat until its internal temperature is between 200 and 210°F (93 and 99°C). This cook typically takes 8 to 10 hours total, but keep in mind that every brisket has different marbling and connectivity tissue, so cooking times can vary.

When your brisket flat hits an internal temperature of 200°F (93°C), start checking it for tenderness. Does your temperature probe go in and out of the brisket flat with ease, or do you still feel some tug? If you still feel resistance, continue cooking until it is probe-tender—the digital temperature probe you are using should slide in and out of the meat as if you were poking a plastic bag full of warm butter. At that time, remove the brisket flat from the Big Green Egg, wrap it in aluminum foil and allow it to rest in an insulated cooler for at least 1 hour before slicing it against the grain and serving.

CHAPTER 3

The Fire Below

GRILLING STEAKS, SEAFOOD AND EVERYTHING IN BETWEEN

Grilling food does not need to be intimidating when cooking with a Big Green Egg. This chapter will help you master the art of grilling different proteins, including fish, poultry, pork and beef. Focusing on controlling the fire below will help you become the expert EGGhead in your neighborhood.

FEEDS: 4 people

APPROXIMATE COOK TIME:
24 hours to marinate,
10 minutes to cook

BIG GREEN EGG SETUP:
Direct

TOOLS AND ACCESSORIES:
Micrograter

1" (2.5-cm) piece fresh ginger, peeled

6 cloves garlic, minced

4 tbsp (60 ml) soy sauce

4 tbsp (60 ml) fish sauce

4 tbsp (55 g) brown sugar

Zest of 1 lime

Juice of 1 lime

4 lb (1.8 kg) bone-in short ribs

Avocado oil or other neutral cooking oil, for grill grates

½ cup (8 g) coarsely chopped fresh cilantro

Thai–Style Marinated Bone–In Short Ribs

I love Korean-style beef short ribs, also known as galbi. For this recipe, I wanted to try something different with this cut. Beef short ribs are thinly cut cross sections of short ribs from a cow. They are so thin you can cook them hot and fast on your Big Green Egg. The combination of flavors with the live-fire char is hard to beat.

Using a micrograter, grate the ginger to a fine paste—you should have about 4 teaspoons (20 g). In a medium bowl, combine the ginger, garlic, soy sauce, fish sauce, brown sugar, lime zest and lime juice.

Place the ribs in a ziplock bag and pour in the marinade, turning the ribs to coat them evenly. Place the bag of ribs in the fridge and let the ribs marinate overnight or up to 24 hours, turning them occasionally.

The next day, set up your Big Green Egg for direct grilling as (described on page 18). Preheat the grill to 450°F (232°C) and let the temperature stabilize. Clean your grill grates and wipe them with a paper towel that has been dipped in the avocado oil. Make sure to wear heat-resistant gloves when you do this.

Remove the ribs from the refrigerator and let them sit at room temperature for 30 minutes while your Big Green Egg preheats. When the Big Green Egg is ready, place the ribs directly on the grill grate and cook them for 3 to 4 minutes. Flip the ribs over and grill them for 3 to 4 minutes on the opposite side. Your target internal temperature is 135°F (57°C) for a medium-rare finish. When that temp is reached, remove the ribs from the Big Green Egg and let them rest for 10 to 15 minutes. Garnish the ribs with the cilantro.

FEEDS: 4 people

APPROXIMATE COOK TIME:
20–30 minutes

BIG GREEN EGG SETUP:
Direct

TOOLS AND ACCESSORIES:
Perforated grilling pan,
mortar and pestle

Avocado oil or other neutral
cooking oil, for grill grates

2-lb (908-g) flat iron steak

Kosher salt

Ground black pepper (ideally
16 mesh)

1 bunch scallions, green parts
discarded

1 Fresno chile

1 habanero chile

3 cloves garlic

2 tbsp (30 ml) cooking oil

2 tbsp (30 g) sugar

2 tbsp (30 ml) fish sauce

2 tbsp (30 ml) fresh lime juice

2 tbsp (2 g) coarsely chopped
fresh cilantro

Flat Iron Steak with Charred Scallion Sauce

I draw inspiration from cuisines and chefs all over the world, but with the increased popularity of TikTok I have found myself inspired by many home cooks and chefs doing their thing online from their homes. One such chef is David Nguyen, as his style of teaching and approachable, delicious food is second to none. This sauce recipe is heavily inspired by his creations; it pairs amazingly with this delicious, fatty cut of beef.

Set up your Big Green Egg for direct grilling (as described on page 18). Preheat the grill to 450°F (232°C) and let the temperature stabilize. Clean your grill grates and wipe them with a paper towel that has been dipped in the avocado oil. Make sure to wear heat-resistant gloves when you do this.

Remove the flat iron steak from the refrigerator 1 hour before you are ready to grill it. Season it with the salt and pepper and let sit at room temperature until you are ready to grill.

Place the white parts of the scallions, Fresno chile, habanero chile and garlic in a medium bowl. Coat them with the cooking oil and season them with salt. When the Big Green Egg has preheated and the temperature is stable, place the vegetables on a perforated grilling pan directly on the grill grate and cook them for 1 to 2 minutes, turning them occasionally, until they are nicely charred. Once the vegetables are charred, transfer them to a cutting board.

Deseed the Fresno chile, but leave the habanero's seeds intact. Mince the chiles, and then place them in a small bowl. Next, cut the scallions into small rounds and add them to the chiles. Place the garlic and sugar in a mortar and pound them with the pestle until they become a paste. Add the fish sauce and lime juice to the paste and stir the ingredients together. Once the sugar is dissolved, add the chile-scallion mixture and cilantro to the sauce, stirring to combine the ingredients.

Place your seasoned flat iron steak on the grill and cook it for 5 to 6 minutes. Flip the steak and grill it for 5 to 6 minutes on the other side, until the meat's internal temperature measures 125°F (52°C). Remove the steak from the Big Green Egg and allow it to rest for 10 minutes before slicing it against the grain and serving it with the charred scallion sauce.

FEEDS: 2–4 people

APPROXIMATE COOK TIME:
20 minutes

BIG GREEN EGG SETUP:
Direct

TOOLS AND ACCESSORIES:
Mortar and pestle

RIB EYE STEAKS

Avocado oil or other neutral cooking oil, for grill grates

2 (1½" [4-cm]-thick) rib eye steaks

1 tbsp (15 ml) olive oil

Kosher salt

Ground black pepper (ideally 16 mesh)

CHILE GREMOLATA

1 bunch Italian flat-leaf parsley

1 clove garlic, minced

1 tsp lemon zest

1 Fresno chile, deseeded and minced

Rib Eye with Chile Gremolata

People often confuse gremolata with chimichurri, and for good reason—they look almost identical. The big difference between the two is that chimichurri uses red wine vinegar and olive oil while gremolata does not. I love to use gremolata on rib eye steaks as the tangy flavor of the gremolata is the perfect complement to the fatty beef.

Load the Big Green Egg with lump charcoal set up for direct grilling (as described on page 18). Preheat your Big Green Egg to 450°F (232°C). Clean your grill grate and wipe it with a paper towel that has been dipped in the avocado oil. Make sure to wear heat-resistant gloves when you do this.

While the Big Green Egg is preheating, take the rib eyes out of the packaging, pat them dry with a paper towel, rub them all over with the olive oil and season them with the salt and pepper.

Next, make your chile gremolata. In a mortar, combine the parsley, garlic, lemon zest and Fresno chile. Grind the ingredients together with the pestle to release all the flavors. Set the gremolata aside while the steaks cook.

Place the rib eyes on the grill grate and cook them for 2 minutes. Flip the steaks and cook them for 2 minutes on the other side. Flip them again and shut the rEGGulator and Draft Door of your Big Green Egg. Let the steaks roast in the Big Green Egg for 3 minutes, or until they measure 130°F (54°C) internally for medium-rare. Pull the steaks from the Big Green Egg, let them rest for 10 minutes and serve them with the chile gremolata.

APPROXIMATE COOK TIME:
1 hour to marinate,
8–10 minutes to cook

BIG GREEN EGG SETUP:
Direct

TOOLS AND ACCESSORIES:
None

Juice of 3 oranges

1 tbsp (6 g) orange zest

Juice of 2 limes

½ cup (120 ml) olive oil

6 cloves garlic, minced

1 cup (16 g) coarsely chopped
fresh cilantro

1 tsp kosher salt, plus more
as needed

1 tsp ground black pepper
(ideally 16 mesh), plus more
as needed

2 tsp (4 g) ground cumin

2 tsp (2 g) dried oregano

4 kurobuta bone-in pork
chops

Avocado oil or other neutral
cooking oil, for grill grates

Mojo Bone–In Pork Chops

*Since moving to Florida, I find myself influenced by regional flavors
from Cuban and other Caribbean cuisines. This pork chop dish draws
heavily on local flavors and produces a delicious grilled treat for your
friends and family.*

In a large bowl, combine the orange juice, orange zest, lime
juice, olive oil, garlic, cilantro, salt, pepper, cumin and oregano
and mix well. Add the pork chops to the marinade and flip them
to coat them evenly. Marinate the pork chops in the refrigerator
for 1 hour.

Remove the pork chops from the marinade, pat them dry with
paper towels and season them with additional salt and pepper.
Let the pork chops sit at room temperature while you set up and
preheat your Big Green Egg.

Load your Big Green Egg with lump charcoal set up for direct
grilling (as described on page 18). Preheat your Big Green Egg
to 450°F (232°C). Clean your grill grate and wipe it with a paper
towel that has been dipped in the avocado oil. Make sure to
wear heat-resistant gloves when you do this.

When the Big Green Egg has preheated and the temperature is
stable, place the pork chops on the grill grate and cook them for
4 minutes. Flip the pork chops and cook them for 4 minutes on
the other side. Check the chops' internal temperature using an
instant-read thermometer. When the pork chops measure 140°F
(60°C), pull them from the Big Green Egg and let them rest for
10 minutes before serving them. The carryover cooking will
bring their internal temperature up to a perfect 145°F (63°C).

FEEDS: 4 people

APPROXIMATE COOK TIME:
10 minutes

BIG GREEN EGG SETUP:
Direct

TOOLS AND ACCESSORIES:
Perforated grilling pan

¼ cup (60 ml) mayonnaise

1 tbsp (15 g) sweet pickle relish

1 tbsp (15 ml) grainy mustard

1 tbsp (15 ml) ketchup

2 tsp (10 ml) hot sauce

4 (6-oz [168-g]) grouper fillets

4 tsp (16 g) your favorite Cajun seasoning (I used Dizzy Pig Bayou-ish Blackening Seasoning)

2 tbsp (30 ml) olive oil

2 tbsp (28 g) butter, softened

4 brioche hamburger buns

4 leaves romaine lettuce

4 slices red onion

Blackened Grouper Sandwich

Living in Florida, I find myself surrounded by fresh seafood. By far the most popular fish served in my area of Florida is grouper. This fish comes in all shapes, sizes and preparations, but a great grouper sandwich is hard to beat. This recipe is easy and will give you a taste of my hometown with every bite.

Set up your Big Green Egg for direct grilling (as described on page 18) and preheat it to 350°F (177°C). Place a perforated grilling pan on your Big Green Egg and let it preheat with the grill.

In a small bowl, combine the mayonnaise, relish, mustard, ketchup and hot sauce. Set this sauce aside for serving.

Wipe the grouper fillets with a paper towel, and then season them with the Cajun seasoning.

When the Big Green Egg has preheated and the temperature is stable, remove the perforated grilling pan using heat-resistant gloves and coat it with olive oil. Place the grilling pan back on the grill grate and add the grouper fillets. Grill them for 4 minutes. Flip the fillets and grill them for 4 minutes on the other side. When the internal temperature of the grouper fillets reaches 140°F (60°C), remove the fillets from the Big Green Egg and let them rest for 5 to 10 minutes.

While the fillets are resting, spread the butter evenly on the split side of each hamburger bun. Place the buns split side down on the grill grate and grill them for 90 seconds, then remove them immediately. Spread the sauce on the buns, place the grouper fillets on top of the sauce and top the fish with the lettuce and onion.

FEEDS: 4 people

APPROXIMATE COOK TIME:
10 minutes

BIG GREEN EGG SETUP:
Direct

TOOLS AND ACCESSORIES:
None

AVOCADO-MANGO SALSA

1 mango, diced

1 avocado, diced

½ red onion, diced

¼ cup (4 g) coarsely chopped fresh cilantro

1 clove garlic, minced

Juice of 1 lime

1 tsp kosher salt

SWORDFISH

1 (1½-lb [681-g]) swordfish fillet

1 tsp olive oil

½ tsp paprika

½ tsp ground cumin

½ tsp garlic powder

½ tsp chili powder

¼ tsp kosher salt

¼ tsp ground black pepper (ideally 16 mesh)

Avocado oil or other neutral cooking oil, for grill grates

Swordfish with Avocado–Mango Salsa

Swordfish is one of my favorite things to grill. This piece of fish is thick and hearty, and it stands up to grilling over direct heat. When the swordfish is paired with my avocado-mango salsa, the flavors of this dish are hard to beat. The salsa can be made in advance and stored in the fridge until needed.

Set up your Big Green Egg for direct grilling (as described on page 18) and preheat it to 350°F (177°C). While the Big Green Egg preheats, make the avocado-mango salsa by combining all of the ingredients for the salsa in a medium bowl. Set the salsa aside until you are ready to serve.

Wipe the swordfish fillet with a paper towel, and then rub it with the olive oil. In a small bowl, mix together the paprika, cumin, garlic powder, chili powder, salt and pepper. Rub the swordfish with the seasoning mix, coating it evenly.

When the Big Green Egg has preheated and the temperature is stable, carefully wipe your grill grate with a paper towel that has been dipped in the avocado oil. Make sure to wear heat-resistant gloves when you do this. Place the swordfish fillet on the grill grate and grill it for 4 minutes. Carefully flip the swordfish over and grill it for 4 minutes on the other side. When the internal temperature of the swordfish fillet reaches 135°F (57°C), remove it from the Big Green Egg and let it rest for 5 to 10 minutes.

Divide the swordfish into four equal portions and top each serving with the avocado-mango salsa.

APPROXIMATE COOK TIME:
20 minutes

BIG GREEN EGG SETUP:
Direct

TOOLS AND ACCESSORIES:
12" (30-cm) cast-iron
skillet

PORK TENDERLOIN

2 (1-lb [454-g]) pork
tenderloins

Kosher salt

Ground black pepper (ideally
16 mesh)

CREAMY MUSHROOM AND
BOURBON SAUCE

2 tbsp (30 ml) olive oil

4 tbsp (56 g) butter

1 lb (454 g) white mushrooms,
thinly sliced

1 yellow onion, diced

8 cloves garlic, minced

1 tsp Dijon mustard

½ tsp Italian seasoning

1 tsp fresh lemon juice

½ cup (120 ml) bourbon

1½ cups (360 ml) heavy cream

Kosher salt, to taste

Ground black pepper, to taste

1–2 tbsp (3–6 g) finely
chopped fresh parsley

Pork Tenderloin with Creamy Mushroom and Bourbon Sauce

Grilled pork tenderloin is one of my favorite things to cook on the Big Green Egg. It is quick, juicy and full of flavor. Paired with a creamy mushroom and bourbon sauce, this tenderloin will quickly become one of your favorite meals to make and serve.

Set up your Big Green Egg for direct grilling (as described on page 18) and preheat it to 375°F (191°C). While the Big Green Egg is preheating, trim the pork tenderloins of any excess fat and silver skin. Season the trimmed tenderloins with the salt and pepper. Let them sit at room temperature until your Big Green Egg is ready.

When the Big Green Egg has preheated and the temperature is stable, place the tenderloins on the grill grate and cook them for 10 minutes. Flip the tenderloins and place a 12-inch (30-cm) cast-iron skillet on the grill grate to preheat while the pork finishes cooking, which will take 10 minutes. When the pork measures 140°F (60°C) internally, remove it from the Big Green Egg and allow it to rest for 20 minutes.

While the pork is resting, make the creamy mushroom and bourbon sauce. Add the olive oil and butter to the preheated cast-iron skillet. Once the butter has melted, add the mushrooms and onion. Sauté them for 10 to 12 minutes, until the mushrooms have released their liquid and the onion is soft and dark yellow in color. Using heat-resistant gloves, remove the cast-iron skillet from the Big Green Egg and stir in the garlic, mustard, Italian seasoning, lemon juice and bourbon. Mix the ingredients together well and return the cast-iron skillet to the Big Green Egg. Pour in the heavy cream and cook the sauce for 3 to 5 minutes, or until the sauce has reduced and thickened. Season the sauce with the salt and black pepper, then stir in the parsley.

Slice the pork tenderloins and serve them with a generous amount of the creamy mushroom and bourbon sauce.

FEEDS: 4–6 people as an app, 2–3 people as a main

APPROXIMATE COOK TIME: 40 minutes

BIG GREEN EGG SETUP: Direct

TOOLS AND ACCESSORIES: None

GLAZE

½ cup (144 g) gochujang paste

¼ cup (60 ml) soy sauce

½ cup (120 ml) honey

2 tbsp (30 ml) rice wine vinegar

2 tbsp (30 ml) fresh lime juice

1 tbsp (15 ml) toasted sesame oil

4 cloves garlic, minced

2 tbsp (30 g) grated fresh ginger

½ stick butter

CHICKEN DRUMSTICKS

6 chicken drumsticks

½ tsp garlic powder

½ tsp kosher salt

½ tsp ground black pepper (ideally 16 mesh)

1 tbsp (15 ml) avocado oil or other neutral cooking oil

Korean–Style Butterflied Chicken Drumsticks

My friend Brad, from Chiles and Smoke™, came up with a trendy recipe for the grill using butterflied chicken drumsticks. I took inspiration from this grilling technique and paired it with a delicious Korean-style glaze, which is perfect for nicely charred and grilled chicken. This is a great appetizer, but you can double the recipe for a complete meal for your friends and family.

Set up your Big Green Egg for direct grilling (as described on page 18) and preheat it to 400°F (204°C).

While the Big Green Egg is preheating, make the glaze. Mix together all of ingredients for the glaze in a small saucepan over medium heat. When the butter has melted and the mixture is warm, use an immersion blender or a countertop blender to blend the mixture to a smooth glaze consistency. Continue cooking the glaze in the saucepan for 20 minutes. Do not bring the glaze to a boil. Reserve ¼ cup (60 ml) of the glaze for a dipping sauce when the chicken is done.

Take the chicken drumsticks out of the packaging and pat them dry with paper towels. Working with one drumstick at a time, place it on your cutting board with the meaty side facing you. Using a sharp knife, cut the meat along one side of the bone, being careful not to slice all the way through. Now make a second cut on the other side of the bone. Fold the meat open like a book, and then lay the drumstick cut side down.

In a small bowl, mix together the garlic powder, salt and pepper to create a dry rub. Brush the drumsticks with the avocado oil, then season them with the dry rub. Place the drumsticks, skin side up, on the grill grate. Close the lid and allow the drumsticks to cook for 5 minutes. Flip the drumsticks and cook them for another 5 minutes. Continue to flip the drumsticks and close the lid every 5 minutes for 20 to 25 minutes, or until the chicken measures between 155 and 160°F (68 to 71°C) internally on an instant-read thermometer.

Once the chicken's internal temperature is between 155 and 160°F (68 to 71°C), baste the drumsticks with the glaze. Leave the top of the Big Green Egg open, allowing the flames from the lump charcoal below to char the outside. Flip the drumsticks, baste them with the glaze again and cook them until the internal temperature is between 170 and 175°F (77 and 79°C). Remove the chicken drumsticks, let them rest for 10 minutes and serve them with the reserved glaze for dipping.

FEEDS: 4 people

APPROXIMATE COOK TIME:
35 minutes

BIG GREEN EGG SETUP:
Two-zone grilling

TOOLS AND ACCESSORIES:
None

FLORENTINE STUFFING

6 oz (168 g) cream cheese, softened

1 tbsp (15 ml) mayonnaise

2 tbsp (30 ml) white wine

2 cloves garlic, minced

¼ tsp kosher salt

2 cups (60 g) baby spinach leaves, coarsely chopped

½ cup (56 g) shredded mozzarella cheese

½ cup (50 g) shredded Parmesan cheese

CHICKEN

4 boneless, skinless chicken breasts (about 1½ lb [681 g] total)

1 tsp kosher salt

½ tsp ground black pepper (ideally 16 mesh)

1 tsp garlic powder

1 tsp ground cumin

1 tsp paprika

Stuffed Florentine Chicken Breasts

When I was growing up, my father owned several steakhouses in the Washington, DC, area. The atmosphere was sophisticated, as was the menu. When I would visit him at one of the restaurants, I would inevitably eat dinner there. Though my dad was well known for his steaks, my favorite thing on the menu was chicken Florentine. I would order it every single time I visited. This recipe is an homage to that experience.

Set up your Big Green Egg for two-zone grilling (as described on page 20) and preheat it to 400°F (204°C).

While the Big Green Egg is preheating, make the Florentine stuffing by combining all of the ingredients for the stuffing in a medium bowl.

Next, slice each chicken breast on one side, being careful not to slice all the way through. Fold the chicken breast open, creating a pocket. Divide the Florentine stuffing into four equal portions. Gently stuff each chicken breast with the Florentine stuffing. Use wooden toothpicks to close and secure the pockets.

In a small bowl, mix together the salt, pepper, garlic powder, cumin and paprika. Sprinkle the outside of the chicken breasts with the seasoning. Let the chicken sit at room temperature until your Big Green Egg is ready.

Place each breast on the indirect side of the grill and cook them for 25 minutes. Start checking the internal temperature of the chicken with an instant-read thermometer after 15 minutes of indirect cooking. When the chicken breasts measure 140°F (60°C), move them to the direct side of the grill and cook them for 4 minutes. Flip the chicken breasts and cook them for 3 to 4 minutes, or until their internal temperature measures 165°F (74°C). Remove the chicken breasts, let them rest for 10 minutes and then slice and serve them.

FEEDS: 4 people

APPROXIMATE COOK TIME:
30 minutes

BIG GREEN EGG SETUP:
Two-zone grilling

TOOLS AND ACCESSORIES:
None

KIMCHI COMPOUND BUTTER

1 stick unsalted butter, softened

1½ oz (42 g) kimchi, finely chopped, with liquid

FILET MIGNON

4 (8-oz [224-g]) filet mignon steaks

2 tbsp (30 ml) olive oil

Kosher salt

Ground black pepper (ideally 16 mesh)

Avocado oil or other neutral cooking oil, for grill grates

Reverse-Seared Filet Mignon with Kimchi Compound Butter

I love steak in any way, shape or form that I can get it! Filet mignon is my wife's favorite cut, so we eat this type of steak fairly often. One thing most people do not know is that even though filet mignon is very tender, it does not pack a lot of flavor. The reason is that this cut isn't as fatty as other cuts, like rib eye and New York strip. So when I grill filet mignon, I add compound butter to give it a little extra fat and flavor. This recipe couldn't be any easier, and the kimchi is such a good counterbalance to the tender and sweet filet mignon.

To make the kimchi compound butter, pulse together the butter and kimchi with its liquid in a food processor until they are combined. Don't overblend the compound butter, as you want some pieces of the kimchi still intact. Now put the softened butter mixture down the center of a sheet of plastic wrap. Next, fold the long edge of plastic wrap that is farthest away from you over the butter, then pull the end plastic closest to you up to produce even pressure, which will squeeze the butter into a uniform log. Finally, grip the ends of the plastic, twist them in opposite directions and tuck them under the butter log to secure it. Chill the compound butter in the refrigerator until you're ready to top the steaks.

Set up your Big Green Egg for two-zone grilling (as described on page 20) and preheat it to 250°F (121°C). While the Big Green Egg preheats, take the steaks out of the packaging and wipe them clean with a paper towel. Rub the steaks with the olive oil, and then season them with the salt and pepper. Let the steaks sit at room temperature until the Big Green Egg is ready.

When the Big Green Egg has preheated and the temperature is stable, carefully oil your grill grate with a paper towel that has been dipped in the avocado oil. Be sure to wear heat-resistant gloves when you do this. Place the seasoned steaks on the indirect side of the grill and cook them for 10 minutes. Flip the steaks and cook them for 10 to 15 minutes. When the internal temperature of the steaks measures 115°F (46°C), pull the steaks from the Big Green Egg and let them rest while you raise the temperature in the Big Green Egg to 450°F (232°C).

When the Big Green Egg is at 450°F (232°C), place the steaks on the direct side of the grill and cook them for 1 to 2 minutes per side to achieve a nice brown color and crust. Remove the steaks from the Big Green Egg and serve each with a slice of the kimchi compound butter on top.

FEEDS: 4–6 people

APPROXIMATE COOK TIME:
20 minutes

BIG GREEN EGG SETUP:
Direct

TOOLS AND ACCESSORIES:
12" (30-cm) cast-iron
skillet

1 red onion, thinly sliced

1 red bell pepper, deseeded
and thinly sliced

1 yellow bell pepper,
deseeded and thinly sliced

2 tbsp (30 ml) olive oil,
divided

1 tsp kosher salt

1 tsp ground black pepper
(ideally 16 mesh)

1 tsp dried oregano

1 tsp dried basil

2 lb (908 g) sweet Italian
sausage links

Grilled Sausage and Peppers

*You wouldn't know it by looking at me, but I am one-fourth Italian
from my father's side of the family. When I was growing up, one of the
dishes I ate when visiting my grandparents was sausage and peppers.
This easy dish is full of flavor and so comforting. You can put this on a
bun with some cheese to make a sandwich, but my guess is you will
eat it right out of the cast-iron skillet!*

Set up your Big Green Egg for raised direct grilling (as described
on page 18) and preheat it to 350°F (177°C). Place a 12-inch
(30-cm) cast-iron skillet on the grill grate while the Big Green
Egg is coming up to temperature. While the Big Green Egg is
preheating, place the onion, red bell pepper and yellow bell
pepper in a large bowl. Add 1 tablespoon (15 ml) of the olive oil
and the salt, pepper, oregano and basil. Toss the vegetables to
coat them in the oil and seasonings.

When the Big Green Egg and cast-iron skillet have preheated,
add the remaining 1 tablespoon (15 ml) of olive oil to the skillet,
then add the seasoned vegetables. Sauté the vegetables for
10 minutes, stirring them frequently. Make sure to wear a
heat-resistant glove during this step to protect your hand.
Remove the skillet from the grill and let the vegetables rest
while you grill the sausages.

Place the sausages on the grill grate and cook them for 8 to
10 minutes, turning them every 2 minutes, until their internal
temperature measures 140°F (60°C). Pull the sausages from the
Big Green Egg and place them in the cast-iron skillet with the
vegetables. Let the sausages rest 10 minutes, then serve the dish
as is or as a filling for your favorite sandwich.

*I love to use Dizzy Pig SPG Herb for the seasoning in this
dish. Skip the seasonings listed and try Dizzy Pig SPG Herb seasoning
if it's available to you.*

FEEDS: 4 people

APPROXIMATE COOK TIME:
30 minutes

BIG GREEN EGG SETUP:
Direct

TOOLS AND ACCESSORIES:
Metal or wooden skewers

HONEY-SRIRACHA GLAZE

1 stick unsalted butter

⅔ cup (160 ml) sriracha

½ cup (120 ml) honey

2 cloves garlic, minced

1 tsp toasted sesame oil

Juice of 1 lime

SHRIMP

1½ lb (681 g) medium shrimp, peeled and deveined

2 tsp (12 g) kosher salt

2 tsp (4 g) ground black pepper (ideally 16 mesh)

2 tsp (6 g) garlic powder

½ tsp paprika

Avocado oil or neutral cooking oil, for grill grate

Lime wedges

Shrimp Skewers with Honey–Sriracha Glaze

Grilled shrimp skewers are always a hit when I am cooking for friends and family. This recipe balances the sweet and the heat perfectly to give you a mouthwatering bite every time. Fast, easy and delicious, this recipe will be one you turn to again and again.

If you are using wooden skewers, soak them in water for 1 hour before putting them on the grill.

In a small saucepan over medium heat, mix together all of the ingredients for the honey-sriracha glaze. Once the ingredients are well combined, reduce the heat to medium-low and simmer the mixture for 20 minutes, or until it has reduced to your desired consistency. Set aside ¼ cup (60 ml) of the glaze for serving.

Set up your Big Green Egg for raised direct grilling (as described on page 18) and preheat it to 450°F (232°C). While the Big Green Egg preheats, take the shrimp out of the packaging. In a small bowl, mix together the salt, pepper, garlic powder and paprika. Sprinkle the shrimp with the spice mixture, coating all the shrimp evenly, then place the shrimp on skewers. Set the skewers aside while the Big Green Egg finishes preheating.

When the Big Green Egg has preheated and the temperature is stable, carefully oil your grill grate with a paper towel that has been dipped in the avocado oil. Be sure to wear heat-resistant gloves when you do this. Place the shrimp skewers on the grill grate and cook them for 3 minutes. Flip the skewers and baste the shrimp with the honey-sriracha glaze. Cook the glazed shrimp for 3 minutes. Flip the shrimp and baste the other side with the glaze, this time making sure the shrimp skewers don't remain on the grill for more than 1 minute. Carefully remove the shrimp skewers from the Big Green Egg. Serve the shrimp with the reserved glaze and the lime wedges.

FEEDS: 6 people

APPROXIMATE COOK TIME:
30 minutes

BIG GREEN EGG SETUP:
Two-zone grilling

TOOLS AND ACCESSORIES:
Metal or wooden skewers

2 lb (908 g) 80/20 ground beef

1 egg

6 snack-sized sticks Colby
Jack cheese

Kosher salt

Ground black pepper (ideally
16 mesh)

12 slices bacon

Hot dog buns (optional)

Bacon–Wrapped Cheeseburger Skewers

I initially hesitated to write a cheeseburger recipe for this section, as there are many cheeseburger recipes out there already. But this recipe is so much fun and makes for a new and unique presentation when cooking and serving cheeseburgers. You never knew you needed a cheeseburger on a stick until you found this recipe. Have fun!

If you are using wooden skewers, soak them in water for 1 hour before putting them on the grill.

Set up your Big Green Egg for two-zone grilling (as described on page 20) and preheat it to 350°F (177°C).

While the Big Green Egg preheats, prep the cheeseburger skewers. In a large bowl, mix the ground beef with the egg until thoroughly combined, then divide the beef into six balls that weigh about 5 ounces (140 g) each. Flatten a ball of ground beef to make a long rectangular shape (long enough to accommodate a cheese stick). Place a cheese stick onto a skewer just far enough so the tip of the skewer is just at the top of the cheese—do not let the skewer poke all the way through the cheese stick. Place the skewered cheese on the flattened beef and form the beef around the cheese stick, sealing it inside the beef completely. Season the outside of the beef with the salt and pepper, then wrap it with 2 slices of the bacon. Repeat this process for the remaining balls of beef and cheese sticks.

When the Big Green Egg has preheated and the temperature is stable, place the bacon-wrapped cheeseburger skewers on the indirect side and cook them for 20 minutes, flipping them two or three times while they cook. When the fat from the bacon is almost rendered, move the skewers to the direct side of the grill and sear the cheeseburger skewers for 30 seconds per side to get the outside slightly charred and crispy. Remove the skewers from the Big Green Egg and allow them to rest for 5 minutes.

Serve the cheeseburger skewers with your favorite condiments or remove the skewers and serve them on hot dog buns for a fun way to eat cheeseburgers!

FEEDS: 4–6 people

APPROXIMATE COOK TIME:
6+ hours to marinate,
25 minutes to cook

BIG GREEN EGG SETUP:
Two-zone grilling

TOOLS AND ACCESSORIES:
None

CHICKEN THIGHS

½ cup (120 ml) olive oil

¾ cup (180 ml) fresh lime juice

12 cloves garlic, coarsely chopped

3 tbsp (54 g) kosher salt

2 tbsp (14 g) paprika

1 tbsp (6 g) ground black pepper (ideally 16 mesh)

1 tbsp (6 g) ground cumin

1 tbsp (3 g) dried oregano

2 tbsp (30 g) sugar

4 lb (1.8 kg) bone-in chicken thighs

AJÍ VERDE

3 jalapeño peppers, deseeded and diced

1 cup (16 g) coarsely chopped fresh cilantro leaves

2 cloves garlic, coarsely chopped

½ cup (120 ml) mayonnaise

¼ cup (60 ml) sour cream

Juice of 1 lime

½ tsp kosher salt

⅛ tsp ground black pepper

2 tbsp (30 ml) olive oil

Grilled Chicken Thighs with Ají Verde

I love eating at my local Peruvian chicken place to get some pollo a la brasa with that delicious green sauce. This recipe is my version of that experience and uses my favorite part of a chicken: the thigh. The sauce is named ají verde (green pepper) and is used as a condiment in Peruvian cuisine. You'll wish you had made more of this sauce when it's gone!

In a blender, combine the olive oil, lime juice, garlic, salt, paprika, pepper, cumin, oregano and sugar and blend the ingredients until they are smooth. Clean the chicken thighs by removing any excess fat and excess skin. Place the cleaned chicken thighs in a large ziplock bag, then pour the marinade all over the chicken. Seal the bag tightly and allow the chicken to marinate in the fridge for 6 hours or overnight.

To make the ají verde, combine all of the ingredients except the olive oil in a medium bowl. Using an immersion blender, blend the ingredients until they are smooth. With the blender still running, drizzle in the olive oil. Alternatively, you can make the ají verde in a countertop blender or food processor. Transfer the ají verde to a covered container and store it the in refrigerator overnight, until you are ready to serve.

The next day, set up your Big Green Egg for two-zone grilling (as described on page 20) and preheat it to 425°F (218°C).

Remove the chicken thighs from the marinade and place them skin side down over the direct-heat side. Grill them for 4 minutes, until you see some nice char and a crust develop on the skin. Flip the thighs over and grill them for 4 minutes on the other side. Next, move the thighs to the indirect side of the grill, ensuring that the thighs are skin side up, and close the top of the Big Green Egg. After 5 minutes, check the internal temperature of the chicken with an instant-read thermometer. When the temperature is at least 165°F (74°C), the chicken thighs are done.

Remove the chicken from the Big Green Egg and let them rest for 10 minutes before serving them with the ají verde.

FEEDS: 4 people

APPROXIMATE COOK TIME:
4 hours to marinate,
5 minutes to cook

BIG GREEN EGG SETUP:
Raised direct grilling

TOOLS AND ACCESSORIES:
None

CHIPOTLE–LIME MARINADE

1 (12-oz [336-g]) can chipotle peppers in adobo sauce

Juice of 2 limes

⅓ cup (80 ml) olive oil

6 cloves garlic, minced

¼ cup (4 g) fresh cilantro stems and leaves

2 tbsp (36 g) kosher salt

1 tbsp (6 g) ground black pepper (ideally 16 mesh)

1 tsp ground cumin

2 tsp (4 g) paprika

2 tsp (6 g) chili powder

STEAK

1 (2-lb [908-g]) skirt steak

Avocado oil or neutral cooking oil, for grill grates

Skirt Steak with Chipotle–Lime Marinade

This recipe will quickly become your go-to for taco night! The marinade uses fresh lime juice, which quickly marinates the thin skirt steak. Easy to make and quick to cook, this recipe will be a solid win next time you're craving steak.

In a blender or food processor, combine all of the ingredients for the chipotle-lime marinade and blend them until they are smooth. Remove the skirt steak from the packaging, wipe it clean with a paper towel, trim away any excess fat and place it in a large ziplock bag. Transfer the marinade to the bag. Let the steak marinate in the fridge for 4 hours before grilling it.

Set up your Big Green Egg for raised direct grilling (as described on page 18) and preheat it to 500°F (260°C). While the Big Green Egg preheats, take the steak out of the marinade and let it come up to room temperature.

When the Big Green Egg has preheated and the temperature is stable, carefully oil your grill grate with a paper towel that has been dipped in the avocado oil. Be sure to wear heat-resistant gloves when you do this. Place the steak on the grill grate and cook it for 2 minutes. Flip the steak and cook it for 2 minutes on the other side. This steak is so thin that 4 minutes is all the time it needs on a hot grill. Pull the steak from the Big Green Egg and let it rest for 5 to 10 minutes. Slice the steak against the grain and serve it immediately.

The convEGGtor Is the Way

ROASTING, BAKING AND MORE

If you think the Big Green Egg is just for smoking and grilling, think again. In this chapter, I will show you how to use indirect cooking methods to bake and roast amazing dishes in your Big Green Egg. Covering everything from poultry to breads and dessert, the recipes in this chapter will make you the talk of the neighborhood.

FEEDS: 4 people

APPROXIMATE COOK TIME:
2–24 hours to dry-brine,
1–1½ hours to cook

BIG GREEN EGG SETUP:
Indirect

TOOLS AND ACCESSORIES:
V-shaped rack and
roasting pan, convEGGtor,
butcher's twine

ROAST CHICKEN

1 (5–6-lb [2.3–2.7-kg]) roasting
chicken

2 tbsp (36 g) kosher salt, plus
more as needed

2 tsp (4 g) ground black
pepper (ideally 16 mesh), plus
more as needed

1 lemon, halved

1 head garlic, cut in half
crosswise

1 bunch fresh thyme

½ yellow onion, quartered

2 tbsp (14 g) unsalted butter,
melted

GRAVY

1 cup (240 ml) chicken stock

2 tbsp (16 g) all-purpose flour

Perfectly Roasted Chicken with Pan Gravy

In my opinion, there is no better comfort food than a perfectly roasted chicken. This recipe is timeless and is made better with the natural flavors coming from the live fire burning inside the Big Green Egg. The only problem I find with this recipe is that I tend to eat most of the chicken while the gravy is cooking!

The day before you plan to roast your chicken, take the chicken out of the packaging and remove the giblets, excess fat and anything else that the butcher left in the cavity of the chicken. Place the chicken on a V-shaped rack that is sitting in a roasting pan and wipe the bird clean with paper towels. In a small bowl, mix together the salt and pepper and apply the mixture evenly all over the chicken and inside the cavity. Place the roasting pan, uncovered, in your fridge and let the chicken dry-brine for 2 to 24 hours.

Set up your Big Green Egg for indirect grilling using the convEGGtor (as described on page 20) and preheat it to 425°F (218°C). While the Big Green Egg preheats, take the roasting pan with the chicken out of the refrigerator. Stuff the cavity of the chicken with the lemon halves by squeezing the juice into the cavity of the chicken and leaving the juiced halves of the lemon inside. Next, stuff the cavity with the garlic, thyme and onion quarters. Brush the outside of the chicken with the butter and season it once again with salt and pepper. Tie the chicken legs together with butcher's twine and tuck the wing tips under the body of the chicken. Leave the chicken at room temperature until the Big Green Egg has preheated.

When the Big Green Egg has preheated and the temperature is stable, place the roasting pan inside and let the chicken roast for 1 to 1½ hours, or until the chicken breast measures at least 165°F (74°C) with an instant-read thermometer and the juice runs clear after probing the meat. When the chicken is done, remove the roasting pan from the Big Green Egg and place the chicken on a cutting board, and then tent the bird with foil. Allow the chicken to rest while you make the pan gravy.

Strain the chicken fat from the roasting pan, reserving 2 tablespoons (30 ml) for the gravy. Heat the chicken stock in a small saucepan over medium-high heat for about 10 minutes, until it starts to reduce. In a small bowl, mix the flour with the reserved chicken fat until the mixture is smooth, then add it to the saucepan. Cook the gravy for 3 to 5 minutes. Reduce the heat to medium-low, bring the gravy to a simmer and season it with salt and pepper to taste.

Serve the chicken with the pan gravy for the ultimate roasted chicken dinner.

FEEDS: 4–6 people

APPROXIMATE COOK TIME:
45 minutes

BIG GREEN EGG SETUP:
Indirect

TOOLS AND ACCESSORIES:
convEGGtor, 12" (30-cm)
cast-iron skillet

2 lb (908 g) pork tenderloin

1 cup (144 g) cornstarch

1 tsp kosher salt

½ tsp ground black pepper
(ideally 16 mesh)

½ tsp paprika

3 tbsp (45 ml) olive oil

2 tbsp (30 ml) fresh lemon
juice

2 cups (480 ml) apple cider

½ cup (120 ml) hot sauce

1 apple, peeled, cored and
thinly sliced

1 cup (113 g) shredded
Cheddar cheese

North Coast Spicy Apple Cider Pork Casserole

When we moved to Gulfport, Florida, we hit the neighbor jackpot with Mark and Lisa from Ohio. They stay here in Gulfport seasonally and are fun people to celebrate life with. Mark is the go-to cook with his group of friends back in Ohio. He made his version of this dish for me, saying it was a favorite of his group of friends. He graciously let me take his dish and reimagine it. I hope you like this version as much as I like his!

Set up your Big Green Egg for indirect grilling using the convEGGtor (as described on page 20) and preheat it to 375°F (191°C). While the Big Green Egg preheats, place a 12-inch (30-cm) cast-iron skillet on the grill grate to preheat with the Big Green Egg.

While the Big Green Egg is preheating, trim the pork tenderloin of extra fat and silver skin. Cut the pork tenderloin into ¾-inch (2-cm)-thick slices, and then pound them into ½-inch (1.3-cm)-thick rounds. In a shallow dish, mix together the cornstarch, salt, pepper and paprika. Dredge each piece of the pork in the seasoned cornstarch and set it aside.

Make sure to wear a heat-resistant glove for the remainder of this recipe to protect your hand while preparing the dish.

When the Big Green Egg and cast-iron skillet have preheated, open the lid carefully and add the olive oil to the cast-iron skillet. Wait until the oil is shimmering, and then, working in batches, place slices of pork in the skillet and cook them for 1 minute per side, until the outside is browned but the pork is not cooked through. Set each batch of pork aside and cook the next batch.

Next, deglaze the skillet with the lemon juice, scraping the bits of pork from the bottom of the skillet. Add the apple cider and hot sauce and mix the ingredients together well. Pour most of the sauce into a small bowl, leaving about a quarter of the sauce in the bottom of the skillet. Remove the skillet from the Big Green Egg and create alternating layers of the pork and sliced apples until they are all used. Pour the reserved sauce over the pork-apple layers. Top the casserole with the Cheddar cheese, cover the skillet and place the skillet back in the Big Green Egg.

Let the casserole cook for 25 minutes, then uncover the skillet and let the casserole cook for 5 to 10 minutes, until the cheese is golden and bubbly. Remove the cast-iron skillet and let the casserole rest for 10 minutes before serving.

FEEDS: 6–8 people

APPROXIMATE COOK TIME:
45 minutes

BIG GREEN EGG SETUP:
Indirect

TOOLS AND ACCESSORIES:
convEGGtor, 5-quart (4.8-L)
cast-iron Dutch oven

RICOTTA TOPPING

1½ cups (369 g) whole-milk
ricotta cheese

½ cup (5 g) coarsely chopped
fresh basil leaves

½ tsp kosher salt

RIGATONI

2 tbsp (30 ml) olive oil,
divided

1 lb (454 g) sweet Italian
sausage, casings removed

½ yellow onion, diced

4 cloves garlic, minced

1 green bell pepper, deseeded
and cut in to 1″ (2.5-cm)
pieces

1 yellow bell pepper, deseeded
and cut in to 1″ (2.5-cm) pieces

1 red bell pepper, deseeded
and cut in to 1″ (2.5-cm)
pieces

1 (25-oz [750-ml]) jar
marinara sauce

¼ tsp kosher salt

Baked Rigatoni with Sausage and Peppers

As you may know by now if you've made some of the other recipes in this book, I am part Italian. So when the holiday season rolls around, Italian food makes a regular appearance on my family's dinner table. I love making this recipe, and everyone is always surprised I make it on the Big Green Egg. It combines two of my favorite dishes: sausage and peppers and baked rigatoni. I hope you like this as much as my family does!

Set up your Big Green Egg for indirect grilling using the convEGGtor (as described on page 20) and preheat it to 400°F (204°C). While the Big Green Egg preheats, place a 5-quart (4.8-L) cast-iron Dutch oven on the grill grate to preheat along with the Big Green Egg.

To make the ricotta topping, combine the ricotta, basil and salt in a small bowl. Whisk the ingredients together until they are thoroughly combined, and then set the topping aside.

Make sure to wear a heat-resistant glove for the remainder of this recipe to protect your hand while preparing the dish.

When the Big Green Egg has preheated, add 1 tablespoon (15 ml) of the olive oil and the sausage to the Dutch oven and cook the sausage for 8 to 10 minutes, stirring it constantly to break it apart and brown the meat. Remove the sausage and set it to the side.

Next, add the remaining 1 tablespoon (15 ml) of olive oil and the onion to the Dutch oven. Cook the onion for 2 minutes, stirring it frequently. Add the garlic and cook the mixture for 1 minute, until the garlic is fragrant. Add the green bell pepper, yellow bell pepper and red bell pepper and continue cooking the vegetables for about 4 minutes, so that the flavors can meld. Pour in the marinara sauce and salt and stir the mixture until everything is fully combined.

1 lb (454 g) rigatoni pasta, cooked and drained (with ½ cup [120 ml] pasta water reserved)

1 cup (100 g) grated Parmesan cheese, divided

1½ cups (168 g) shredded mozzarella cheese

Add the rigatoni to the Dutch oven and sprinkle it with ½ cup (50 g) of the Parmesan cheese. Stir the mixture to combine the pasta and the Parmesan cheese with the other ingredients. Add the reserved pasta water to the mixture, which will thin the sauce for you.

Next, spoon the ricotta topping evenly over the top of the pasta mixture. Cover the ricotta with the mozzarella and remaining ½ cup (50 g) of Parmesan cheese. Close the lid of the Big Green Egg and bake the pasta for about 20 minutes. When the top is bubbly and nicely browned, remove the Dutch oven from the Big Green Egg and allow the baked rigatoni to rest for 10 minutes before serving it.

FEEDS: 6–8 people

APPROXIMATE COOK TIME:
24 hours to dry-brine,
1½ hours to cook

BIG GREEN EGG SETUP:
Indirect

TOOLS AND ACCESSORIES:
Butcher's twine,
convEGGtor, roasting pan
and V-shaped rack

1 (4-lb [1.8-kg]) top round
beef roast

4 tsp (24 g) kosher salt

¼ cup (60 ml) olive oil

6 cloves garlic, minced

2 tbsp (4 g) finely chopped
fresh rosemary

2 tsp (4 g) ground black
pepper

½ cup (120 ml) beef broth

½ cup (120 ml) red wine

1 yellow onion, thinly sliced

1 tbsp (9 g) cornstarch

1 tbsp (15 ml) water

Homestyle Roast Beef

This savory roast beef is the perfect centerpiece for your dinner table. The drippings created by the top round as it cooks marry well with the stock, producing an amazing gravy to serve with the sliced roast. The best part of this dish is that the leftovers can be sliced thinly for sandwiches the next day!

The day before you plan to cook your roast, take the top round out of the packaging and wipe it clean with a paper towel. Cover the outside of the roast with the salt and tie the roast with butcher's twine. Set a wire rack on a baking sheet, then place the seasoned roast on the rack. Transfer the baking sheet, uncovered, to the fridge and let the meat dry-brine for 24 hours.

The next day, take the baking sheet with the top round roast out of the refrigerator 1 hour before you plan to cook the roast.

Set up your Big Green Egg for indirect grilling using the convEGGtor (as described on page 20) and preheat it to 250°F (121°C). While the Big Green Egg preheats, mix the olive oil with the garlic, rosemary and pepper in a small bowl. Place the roast in a roasting pan fitted with a V-shaped rack. Pour the broth and red wine into the roasting pan and add the onion. Rub the oil-herb mixture all over the outside of the roast, and then let the roast sit in the roasting pan while your Big Green Egg comes up to temperature.

When the Big Green Egg has preheated and the temperature is stable, place the beef inside and cook until the center measures 115°F (46°C) on an instant-read thermometer. Typically, this takes 15 minutes per pound, or 1 hour for a 4-pound (1.8-kg) roast.

Using heat-resistant gloves, remove the roasting pan from the Big Green Egg and set it aside while you increase the temperature of the Big Green Egg to 475°F (246°C). When the heat reaches 475°F (246°C), place it back inside and let the roast cook for 10 to 15 minutes, until the outside is nice and brown and the internal temperature is 135°F (57°C).

Pull the roasting pan out of the Big Green Egg, place the roast beef on a cutting board and let it rest for 20 to 30 minutes. Using a mesh strainer, strain the pan drippings into a small saucepan. Warm the strained liquid from the roasting pan over medium heat. In a small bowl, mix the cornstarch with the water and whisk that mixture into the drippings. Reduce the heat to medium-low and let the gravy simmer for 10 to 20 minutes, until it has thickened. Slice the roast beef and serve it with the gravy.

FEEDS: 12–24 people

APPROXIMATE COOK TIME: 2 hours

BIG GREEN EGG SETUP: Indirect

TOOLS AND ACCESSORIES: convEGGtor, meat trussing needle, butcher's twine, wire baking rack

PEACH GLAZE

2 cups (340 g) peach preserves

2 tbsp (30 ml) honey

2 tbsp (28 g) light brown sugar

2 tbsp (30 ml) apple cider vinegar

2 tbsp (30 ml) Worcestershire sauce

Kosher salt, to taste

Ground black pepper, to taste

PORK CROWN

2 (6-lb [2.7-g]) bone-in racks of pork

2 tbsp (30 ml) olive oil

3–4 tbsp (36–48 g) your favorite BBQ Rub (I used Dizzy Pig Raging River)

Kurobuta Pork Crown Roast with Peach Glaze

This recipe is a little more involved than some of the others in this book, but trust me—it is well worth the effort. This is by far the most beautiful centerpiece to a holiday meal. If you are looking for that showstopper moment, this is the recipe for you. I order the kurobuta bone-in pork roast from Snake River Farms, but another kind of heritage-breed pork crown from your local butcher or grocery store will work great.

Set up your Big Green Egg for indirect grilling using the convEGGtor (as described on page 20) and preheat it to 350°F (177°C). While your Big Green Egg is preheating, make the peach glaze and prepare the pork crown.

To make the peach glaze, combine the peach preserves, honey, brown sugar, vinegar and Worcestershire sauce in a small saucepan over medium heat. Bring the glaze to a light boil, then reduce the heat to medium-low and let the glaze simmer for 20 minutes. Remove the glaze from the heat and season it with the salt and pepper. Reserve ¼ cup (60 ml) of the glaze and set it aside until the pork roast is done.

To make the pork crown, you'll need to visit your local butcher and ask them to make the crown; or, if you are feeling adventurous, buy a meat trussing needle and some butcher's twine and do it yourself!

To make the crown yourself, start with two frenched bone-in pork roasts and put them end to end next to one another, with the bones facing the same direction. Thread the trussing needle with butcher's twine and run the needle through one end of the first pork roast and into the opposing end of the other. Remove the needle and gently tie a knot to hold the two pieces of pork roast together. Do this two or three more times, evenly spacing the knots apart, until you have secured one end of pork roast to the other. Now take the opposite end of the pork roast and bend both ends of the roast to meet each other in order to form the "crown." Using the trussing needle, connect the ends in the same way you did the opposite ends. Now you have a beautiful pork crown roast ready to be seasoned.

Place the crown roast on a well-oiled wire baking rack. In a small bowl, mix the olive oil with your BBQ rub and slather the mixture all over the pork roast. When the Big Green Egg is at temperature, put the wire rack holding your crown roast in the Big Green Egg. Cook the pork for 2 hours, or until the internal temperature measures 135°F (57°C). Glaze the roast with the peach glaze and cook the roast for 5 to 10 minutes, until the internal temperature measures 145°F (63°C).

Remove the crown, let it rest for 5 minutes and then slice it and serve it with the reserved peach glaze.

FEEDS: 2–4 people

APPROXIMATE COOK TIME:
15 minutes

BIG GREEN EGG SETUP:
Indirect

TOOLS AND ACCESSORIES:
convEGGtor, 12" (30-cm) ceramic pizza stone, wooden pizza peel, metal pizza peel

LIME CREMA

½ cup (120 ml) mayonnaise

¼ cup (60 ml) sour cream

Juice of ½ lime

PIZZA

1 lb (454 g) prepared refrigerated pizza dough

2 tbsp (30 ml) olive oil

6 cloves garlic, minced

8 oz (224 g) shredded mozzarella cheese

1 ear corn, grilled and kernels removed

1 poblano pepper, grilled, deseeded and coarsely chopped

FOR SERVING

¼ cup (30 g) crumbled cotija cheese

1 tsp smoked paprika

4 scallions, green portions coarsely chopped and white parts discarded

¼ cup (4 g) coarsely chopped fresh cilantro

Lime wedges

Elotes Pizza with Lime Crema

This is a great pizza option for the vegetarians in your life. The concept is simple: This is what happens when Mexican street corn meets pizza. This pizza is so good you will want to make it again and again.

Set up your Big Green Egg for indirect grilling using the convEGGtor (as described on page 20) and preheat it to 450°F (232°C). To cook the pizza without burning the crust, I have a trick for you: Take three 12 x 12–inch (30 x 30–cm) pieces of aluminum foil and form small balls with them. Place them on the grill grate and then place the 12-inch (30-cm) ceramic pizza stone on top of the foil balls. The small bit of airflow underneath the pizza stone will allow the stone to heat with the Big Green Egg but not get hot enough to burn the crust as it cooks. As the Big Green Egg and the pizza stone preheat, make your lime crema.

In a small bowl, mix together all the ingredients for the lime crema until the mixture is smooth. Transfer the crema to a plastic squeeze bottle if you have one and place it in the fridge to chill until your pizza is ready.

Shape your pizza dough on a well-floured surface until you have a 12-inch (30-cm) circular pizza crust. In a small bowl, mix together the olive oil and garlic and spread the mixture evenly across the dough. Sprinkle the mozzarella across the surface of the oiled dough, and then top it with the grilled corn and poblano pepper.

When the Big Green Egg and pizza stone have preheated, launch the pizza onto the stone using a wooden pizza peel. Close the lid of the Big Green Egg and cook the pizza for 5 minutes before checking the crust. Using a metal pizza peel, gently lift the edge of your pizza crust and look at the bottom to see if it has set and if it has browned. If the crust has browned more on one side, use the metal pizza peel to turn the pizza slightly in order to cook the crust evenly across the bottom. It could be another 5 to 10 minutes before the pizza is ready. You will know it's ready when the cheese on top is bubbly and starting to brown and the crust underneath has browned evenly.

Take the pizza off your Big Green Egg using the metal pizza peel and transfer the pizza to a cutting board. Now sprinkle the top of the pizza with the cotija cheese and smoked paprika. Garnish the pizza with the scallions and cilantro, then drizzle the lime crema over the top of the pizza. Serve the pizza with the lime wedges.

FEEDS: 2–4 people

APPROXIMATE COOK TIME:
15 minutes

BIG GREEN EGG SETUP:
Indirect

TOOLS AND ACCESSORIES:
convEGGtor, 12″ (30-cm) ceramic pizza stone, wooden pizza peel, metal pizza peel

PESTO

2 cups (48 g) loosely packed fresh basil leaves

⅓ cup (45 g) pine nuts

4 cloves garlic, minced

½ cup (50 g) grated Parmesan cheese

½ cup (120 ml) extra-virgin olive oil

¼ tsp kosher salt

⅛ tsp ground black pepper

BALSAMIC VINEGAR GLAZE

½ cup (120 ml) balsamic vinegar

The Buddha's Steakhouse Pizza

I made this pizza for a convention I was cooking at back in October 2021. I must have cooked 80 of these pizzas over a two-day period! This was such a popular item at our Big Green Egg tent that people came back for a slice multiple times during the two-day conference. You can make your own dough, but I find that using a good-quality store-bought dough reduces the number of moving pieces, allowing you to focus on making the best pizza ever using your Big Green Egg.

Set up your Big Green Egg for indirect grilling using the convEGGtor (as described on page 20) and preheat it to 450°F (232°C). To cook the pizza without burning the crust, follow the aluminum foil trick described on page 126. Place the 12-inch (30-cm) ceramic pizza stone on the aluminum foil balls so that it preheats along with the Big Green Egg.

While the Big Green Egg is coming to temperature, make the pesto. Place the basil leaves and pine nuts in a food processor and pulse until they are roughly combined. Add the garlic along with Parmesan cheese and pulse a few more times, until the ingredients are well combined. Make sure to scrape the sides of the food processor's bowl to incorporate all of the ingredients into the pesto. Next, run the food processor on the slowest speed and slowly add the olive oil to help emulsify the ingredients. Stop this process every now and again to scrape the bowl of the food processor, ensuring all of the ingredients are combined. Season the pesto sauce with the salt and pepper, and you are now ready to make the pizza.

In a small saucepan over medium heat, bring the balsamic vinegar to a gentle boil. When the vinegar is at a gentle boil, reduce the heat to low and simmer the vinegar for 10 to 15 minutes, stirring it occasionally, until it has reduced by half. When the vinegar lightly coats the back of a spoon, it is ready!

(continued)

The Buddha's Steakhouse Pizza (continued)

PIZZA

1 lb (454 g) prepared refrigerated pizza dough

8 oz (224 g) shredded mozzarella cheese

½ red onion, sliced very thinly

1 lb (454 g) New York strip steak, cooked to rare (120°F [49°C]) and thinly sliced

2 tbsp (16 g) crumbled blue cheese

½ cup (15 g) loosely packed baby arugula

Shape your pizza dough on a well-floured surface until you have a 12-inch (30-cm) circular pizza. Spread some of the pesto on the dough (reserving the remaining pesto for other pizzas) and sprinkle the mozzarella evenly on top of the pesto. Now lay the slices of red onion across the top of the cheese. Finally, place the thinly sliced steak evenly across the top of the pizza.

When the Big Green Egg and pizza stone have preheated, launch the pizza onto the stone using a wooden pizza peel. Close the lid of the Big Green Egg and cook the pizza, undisturbed, for 5 minutes. Using a metal pizza peel, gently lift of the edge of your pizza crust and look at the bottom to see if it has set and if it has browned. If the crust has browned more on one side, use the metal pizza peel to turn the pizza slightly to cook the crust evenly across the bottom. It could be another 5 to 10 minutes before the pizza is ready. You will know it's ready when the cheese on top is bubbly and starting to brown and the crust underneath has browned evenly.

Remove the pizza from the Big Green Egg with the metal pizza peel, top it with the blue cheese and baby arugula and then drizzle it with the balsamic glaze.

FEEDS: 8 people

APPROXIMATE COOK TIME:
3–5 hours

BIG GREEN EGG SETUP:
Indirect

TOOLS AND ACCESSORIES:
convEGGtor, wire baking
rack, 5-quart (4.8-L) cast-
iron Dutch oven

MEATBALLS

8 oz (224 g) ground beef

8 oz (224 g) ground pork

8 oz (224 g) ground veal

1 cup (100 g) grated
Parmesan cheese

½ tsp kosher salt

½ tsp ground black pepper

1 slice white bread, broken
up into small pieces

½ tsp garlic powder

½ tsp onion powder

2 tbsp (6 g) minced fresh
parsley

2 eggs

Noni's Meatballs and Sunday Gravy

Growing up with an Italian grandmother was a magical thing for an aspiring foodie. Every Christmas and Easter, my house would be filled with wonderful aromas as my Noni took over the kitchen. Her Sunday gravy is my standard when I think of tomato sauce, and I am happy to share that recipe—and the one for her meatballs—with all of you. The live-fire cooking environment of the Big Green Egg brings a whole new dimension of flavor to this classic meal.

Set up your Big Green Egg for indirect grilling using the convEGGtor (as described on page 20) and preheat it to 350°F (177°C). Place a 5-quart (4.8-L) cast-iron Dutch oven in the Big Green Egg and let that preheat along with the Big Green Egg. While the Big Green Egg and Dutch oven are preheating, make your meatballs.

In a large bowl, mix together all of the ingredients for the meatballs until they are well combined. Form the mixture into medium-sized balls. Place the meatballs on a greased wire baking rack. Once the Big Green Egg has preheated, place the rack with the meatballs on the grill grate (staying clear of the Dutch oven inside) and cook the meatballs for 30 minutes, flipping the meatballs halfway through the cooking time. When the meatballs are nicely browned, they are done. Remove the wire rack of meatballs from the Big Green Egg and set it aside while you make the Sunday gravy.

SUNDAY GRAVY

2 tbsp (30 ml) olive oil

1 yellow onion, diced

4 cloves garlic, minced

1 (28-oz [784-g]) can San Marzano tomatoes

1 (28-oz [840-ml]) can tomato purée

2 (15-oz [450-ml]) cans tomato sauce

1 cup (240 ml) water

1 (6-oz [168-g]) can tomato paste

½ tsp dried basil

½ tsp dried oregano

1 dried bay leaf

1 tsp kosher salt

1 tsp ground black pepper

Add the olive oil, onion and garlic to the preheated Dutch oven. Sauté them for 2 to 3 minutes, stirring them frequently, until the onion is tender and the garlic is fragrant. Add the San Marzano tomatoes, tomato purée, tomato sauce and water. Mix the ingredients well and bring the sauce to a boil. Close the rEGGulator and Draft Door of your Big Green Egg so that both vents are 90 percent closed. Doing this will gradually reduce the heat inside the grill. Allow the sauce to simmer for 30 minutes.

Now add the tomato paste, basil, oregano, bay leaf, salt and pepper to the sauce. Mix the ingredients into the sauce, then add the meatballs to the sauce. Cover the Dutch oven and simmer the sauce for 2 to 4 hours (the longer you wait, the better the flavor is). When you are ready, serve the meatballs and sauce over pasta for an amazing Italian-inspired meal.

FEEDS: 6 people

APPROXIMATE COOK TIME:
1 hour

BIG GREEN EGG SETUP:
Direct and indirect

TOOLS AND ACCESSORIES:
convEGGtor, 9 x 13" (23 x
33-cm) casserole dish

1 ear corn, husked and
cleaned

1 lb (454 g) poblano peppers

2 eggs, separated

2 tbsp (16 g) all-purpose flour

¼ tsp kosher salt

¼ tsp baking soda

12 oz (336 g) fresh spinach,
cooked and squeezed to
remove excess water

8 oz (224 g) shredded
Monterey Jack cheese

8 oz (224 g) shredded sharp
Cheddar cheese

½ cup (8 g) coarsely chopped
fresh cilantro

Chile Relleno Casserole

This simple casserole is a favorite of mine when I am craving something delicious. The freshly roasted ingredients bring out amazing flavors you will crave time and time again. This is the perfect dish for any table featuring Tex-Mex food.

Start by roasting the vegetables. To do that, set up your Big Green Egg for direct grilling (as described on page 18) and preheat it to 400°F (204°C). When the Big Green Egg is ready, roast the corn by placing it directly on the grill grate. Cook the corn for 6 to 8 minutes, turning it frequently, until it is nicely browned. Pull the corn off the grill grate and set it aside to cool. Now roast the poblano peppers for 3 minutes per side, until the skin is blackened and blistered. Place the roasted peppers in a covered container, so that the steam will help loosen the skin. Finally, peel and deseed the peppers, cut them so they're split open like a book and set them to the side.

Place the convEGGtor in your Big Green Egg to set it up for indirect grilling. Raise the temperature in the Big Green Egg to 475°F (246°C).

While the Big Green Egg is coming to its new temperature, make the relleno batter and assemble the casserole. In a medium bowl, whisk both of the egg whites until they become foamy, then add one of the egg yolks, flour, salt and baking soda. Mix the ingredients together to form the batter. Set the batter aside until your casserole is assembled.

To assemble the casserole, place a layer of roasted chiles (opened like a book) on the bottom of a 9 x 13–inch (23 x 33–cm) casserole dish. Top the chiles with the spinach and some of the Monterey Jack cheese and Cheddar cheese. Place another layer of chiles on top of that and cover them with the roasted corn, cilantro and more of the Monterey Jack and Cheddar. Finally, add one last layer of chiles and the remaining Monterey Jack and Cheddar and top layer that with the relleno batter.

Place the casserole in the preheated Big Green Egg and cook it for about 45 minutes, until the cheesy topping is nicely browned and bubbling around the edges. Remove the casserole from the Big Green Egg and let it rest for 15 to 20 minutes before serving it.

FEEDS: 4 people

APPROXIMATE COOK TIME: 20 minutes

BIG GREEN EGG SETUP: Indirect

TOOLS AND ACCESSORIES: convEGGtor, 13" (33-cm) rectangular drip pan

1 tbsp (15 ml) olive oil

1 (1½-lb [681-g]) skin-on salmon fillet

3 cups (273 g) broccoli florets

3 tbsp (42 g) brown sugar

3 tbsp (45 ml) soy sauce

3 tbsp (45 ml) toasted sesame oil

1 tbsp (15 ml) chili-garlic sauce

1 tbsp (15 ml) rice wine vinegar

2 cloves garlic, minced

1 tsp minced fresh ginger

1 tbsp (9 g) toasted sesame seeds

4 scallions, green parts thinly sliced and white parts discarded

One-Pan Roasted Asian Salmon and Broccoli

This is a go-to meal for my family during the week. This one-pan dinner is super easy to make and packed with flavor. From start to finish, this entire meal takes less than an hour to make and serve. Balancing sweet and savory, this dish will have your tastebuds dancing.

Set up your Big Green Egg for indirect grilling using the convEGGtor (as described on page 20) and preheat it to 400°F (204°C). While the Big Green Egg is preheating, start prepping the ingredients.

Line a 13-inch (33-cm) rectangular drip pan with aluminum foil. Rub the foil with the olive oil and place the salmon fillet in the pan skin side down. Arrange the broccoli around the salmon and set the drip pan aside.

In a small bowl, combine the brown sugar, soy sauce, sesame oil, chili-garlic sauce, rice wine vinegar, garlic and ginger. Mix the ingredients well to combine them, and then spoon most of the sauce over the salmon fillet, drizzling it lightly over the broccoli too.

When the Big Green Egg has preheated, place the pan with the salmon and broccoli inside. Roast the salmon and broccoli for 15 to 20 minutes, or until the salmon reaches 145°F (63°C) internally. Remove the pan and garnish the salmon and broccoli with the toasted sesame seeds and scallions.

FEEDS: 6 people

APPROXIMATE COOK TIME:
2 hours to prep dough,
8–10 minutes to cook

BIG GREEN EGG SETUP:
Indirect/baking

TOOLS AND ACCESSORIES:
convEGGtor, 12″ (30-cm)
ceramic pizza stone

1⅓ cups (320 ml) warm water
(104°F [40°C]), divided

2 tsp (8 g) active dry yeast

1 tsp sugar

3 cups (375 g) all-purpose
flour, divided

1 tsp kosher salt

2 tbsp (30 ml) extra-virgin
olive oil

Homemade Pita Bread

Nothing is quite as satisfying as freshly made pita bread. Warm, soft and chewy, this recipe is my go-to bread for dips and sandwiches. You can make the pita bread in advance and freeze the rounds for up to six months. Your next batch of hummus will thank you.

Pour 1 cup (240 ml) of the warm water into a large nonreactive bowl (such as a glass bowl), and then stir in the yeast and sugar until they have dissolved. Next, mix in ½ cup (63 g) of the flour and mix the ingredients well. Place the uncovered bowl in a warm place for 15 minutes, until you see the mixture start to bubble.

When you see the dough bubbling, it is time to add the salt, olive oil and 2 cups (250 g) of the remaining flour. Continue to mix until you work in all the bits and pieces in the bowl. Dust a work surface with the remaining ½ cup (63 g) of flour. Dump the shaggy dough mixture onto the floured surface and knead the dough for up to 10 minutes, or until the dough ball has a smooth texture and consistency. At this point, place your dough in a medium bowl lightly greased with olive oil, tossing the dough around a bit to ensure the dough is coated in the oil. Next, cover the bowl with plastic wrap and then with a kitchen towel. Let the dough rise for 45 to 60 minutes, until it has doubled in size.

Punch down the dough to deflate it, and then divide it into six balls. Place each ball side by side on a baking sheet, and then cover the baking sheet with plastic wrap. Let the covered dough balls sit for 30 minutes. Next, roll each of the dough balls into circles about 6 inches (15 cm) in diameter and ⅛ inch (3 mm) thick. Cover the dough rounds with a wet paper towel as you set up your Big Green Egg.

Set up your Big Green Egg for indirect grilling using the convEGGtor (as described on page 20) and preheat it to 500°F (260°C). Place three large balls of aluminum foil on the grill grate's surface in a triangular pattern, then place a 12-inch (30-cm) ceramic pizza stone on top of the balls. Allow the stone to preheat with the Big Green Egg.

Once the temperature is stable at 500°F (260°C), place a dough round on the pizza stone. Close the dome of the Big Green Egg and cook the pita dough round for 8 to 10 minutes, flipping the dough halfway through. You are looking for the top to brown slightly and the pita pocket to be fully inflated; that's how you know it's ready to pull the bread off the pizza stone. Repeat this process with the remaining pita dough rounds until all are cooked.

FEEDS: 8 people

APPROXIMATE COOK TIME:
7–9 hours to prep dough,
30 minutes to cook

BIG GREEN EGG SETUP:
Indirect/baking

TOOLS AND ACCESSORIES:
convEGGtor, 5-quart (4.8-L)
cast-iron Dutch oven

3 cups (375 g) all-purpose
flour, plus more as needed

1 tsp kosher salt

¾ tsp active dry yeast

1½ cups (360 ml) warm water
(104°F [40°C])

1 cup (113 g) shredded
Cheddar cheese

1 jalapeño, thinly sliced

Cast-Iron Cheddar and Jalapeño Bread

This is one of my favorite recipes to make at an EGGfest. Everyone loves freshly baked bread, and watching a loaf like this come off the Big Green Egg is impressive. Served with some softened butter, this bread will quickly become a favorite recipe of yours too.

In a large bowl, combine the flour, salt and yeast, mixing until the ingredients are combined. Make a well in the middle of the flour mixture, then slowly add the warm water. Stir this mixture until a shaggy dough ball forms. Now cover the bowl and set it in a warm place, allowing the dough to double in size—this will take 6 to 8 hours.

Lightly dust a work surface with additional flour and transfer the dough to the prepared work surface (the dough will deflate during this process). Now start adding the Cheddar cheese and jalapeño slices as you fold the dough over itself three or four times to incorporate the cheese and jalapeño. When the dough is ready, shape it into a ball and cover it with a kitchen towel. Let this dough ball rise until it is doubled in size, which will take 1 to 2 hours.

Set up your Big Green Egg for indirect grilling using the convEGGtor (as described on page 20) and preheat it to 450°F (232°C). Place a 5-quart (4.8-L) cast-iron Dutch oven—with its lid on—onto the grill grate and let the Dutch oven preheat with the Big Green Egg. When the temperature is stable, uncover the dough ball and place it onto a piece of parchment paper. Wearing heat-resistant gloves, carefully remove the preheated Dutch oven from the Big Green Egg and place the parchment paper with the dough ball inside the Dutch oven. Score the top of the dough ball with a sharp knife, forming a large X on top—this will help when the bread starts rapidly expanding. Cover the Dutch oven with the preheated lid.

Place the Dutch oven back in the Big Green Egg and bake the bread for 30 minutes. Next, wearing heat-resistant gloves, remove the lid of the Dutch oven and bake the bread for 15 minutes, until the top is nice and brown. Wearing heat-resistant gloves, remove the Dutch oven from your Big Green Egg and, using the parchment paper, remove the bread. Place the loaf on a wire baking rack to cool for at least 15 minutes before slicing and serving it.

FEEDS: 6–8 people

APPROXIMATE COOK TIME:
1 hour

BIG GREEN EGG SETUP:
Indirect/baking

TOOLS AND ACCESSORIES:
convEGGtor, 12" (30-cm)
cast-iron skillet

1 tbsp (14 g) butter

1 (24-oz [672-g]) can peaches in syrup, drained

1 (15-oz [420-g]) box yellow cake mix

1 (12-oz [360-ml]) can Sprite®

1 tsp ground cinnamon

Campground Peach Spoon Cake

My neighbor Mark uses this recipe every summer when he's camping in Ohio with his friends. He showed me how he makes this cake using his grill at the campground. I took his recipe and tweaked it just enough to work on a Big Green Egg. This recipe is so good you will wish you had made a second batch. I cannot wait to make this at EGGtoberfest!

Set up your Big Green Egg for indirect grilling using the convEGGtor (as described on page 20) and preheat it to 350°F (177°C). While the Big Green Egg preheats, coat a 12-inch (30-cm) cast-iron skillet with the butter and set the skillet aside.

Pour the peaches into the buttered cast-iron skillet. In a large bowl, gently combine the cake mix and Sprite. Pour the mixture into the cast-iron skillet and sprinkle the cinnamon on top.

When the Big Green Egg has preheated and the temperature is stable, carefully place the cast-iron skillet inside and let the cake bake for 45 to 60 minutes. You will know when the cake is done when you poke the cake with a toothpick and it comes out clean with no wet batter. Let the cake cool for 5 to 10 minutes, then spoon out servings to happy friends and family who have been anxiously waiting.

FEEDS: 8 people

APPROXIMATE COOK TIME:
45 minutes

BIG GREEN EGG SETUP:
Indirect/baking

TOOLS AND ACCESSORIES:
convEGGtor, 9" (23-cm)
pie pan

1 cup (240 ml) dark corn
syrup (I use Karo® brand)

½ cup (100 g) plus 1 tbsp
(15 g) sugar, divided

3 tbsp (42 g) butter

3 eggs

1 tsp pure vanilla extract

⅛ tsp kosher salt

1 cup (112 g) pecan halves

1 (9" [23-cm]) refrigerated
prepared pie crust

1 tbsp (8 g) all-purpose flour

Grammy Red's Pecan Pie

When I was growing up, there were certain recipes my mother (a.k.a. Grammy Red to my kids) would make that led others to hold her in the highest esteem. Her pecan pie is the best I have ever eaten. Every holiday season, I would anxiously await this pie to be served with her homemade whipped cream. Thankfully, I got this recipe from her before she passed away in 2001. I hope you like this one as much as I do.

Set up your Big Green Egg for indirect grilling using the convEGGtor (as described on page 20) and preheat it to 375°F (191°C). While the Big Green Egg is coming up to temperature, make the pie.

In a small saucepan over medium heat, mix together the corn syrup and ½ cup (100 g) of the sugar. Bring the mixture to a slight simmer, watching for the sugar to completely dissolve. Next, add the butter, constantly stirring the mixture to work the butter in as it melts. In a medium bowl, loosely beat the eggs, then slowly whisk in the corn syrup–sugar mixture. Mix in the vanilla, salt and pecan halves.

Add your pie crust to a 9-inch (23-cm) pie pan, fluting the edges of the crust. Next, combine the flour and remaining 1 tablespoon (15 g) of sugar in a small bowl, and then sprinkle the mixture evenly over the bottom of the crust. (This step is a trick my mom would use to prevent the dough from getting soggy when she added the filling.) Now pour the pecan filling into the fluted pie crust evenly.

Once the Big Green Egg is stable at 375°F (191°C), place the pie pan on the grill grate and bake the pie for 45 minutes. When the top is well browned and the filling is set, take the pie out of the Big Green Egg and let it cool for 15 to 30 minutes before slicing and serving it.

FEEDS: 6–8 people

APPROXIMATE COOK TIME:
30 minutes

BIG GREEN EGG SETUP:
Indirect/baking

TOOLS AND ACCESSORIES:
convEGGtor, 12″ (30-cm)
cast-iron skillet

APPLE FILLING

5 Braeburn or Golden Delicious apples, peeled and thinly sliced

¼ cup (55 g) packed light brown sugar

2 tbsp (16 g) all-purpose flour

2 tsp (6 g) ground cinnamon

½ tsp ground nutmeg

1 tsp kosher salt

1 tbsp (15 ml) fresh lemon juice

1 tsp pure vanilla extract

3 tbsp (45 ml) bourbon

CRUMBLE TOPPING

½ cup (63 g) all-purpose flour

⅔ cup (60 g) old-fashioned oats

1 cup (220 g) packed brown sugar

2½ tsp (8 g) ground cinnamon

½ tsp ground cardamom

½ tsp ground nutmeg

¼ tsp salt

¼ cup (31 g) pecans

½ cup (112 g) cold butter, cut into cubes

Mrs. Buddha's Apple Crumble

When I first started cooking at EGGfests around the country, I was deficient in the dessert category. Like most chefs, I have spent my culinary career focused on the savory side of things. My wife, a.k.a. Mrs. Buddha, loves to bake and helped me create this delicious apple crumble recipe for an EGGfest many years ago. I am happy to share our work with you here.

Set up the Big Green Egg for indirect grilling using the convEGGtor (as described on page 20) and preheat it to 375°F (191°C). While the Big Green Egg is preheating, start prepping the apple filling.

Place all of the ingredients for the apple filling in a large bowl and mix everything well to combine. Now pour the filling into a 12-inch (30-cm) cast-iron skillet.

To make the crumble topping, place the flour, oats, brown sugar, cinnamon, cardamom, nutmeg, salt and pecans in a food processor. Pulse until the nuts are chopped and the mixture is combined. While the mixture is still in the food processor, add the butter and pulse again until the mixture looks like a wet, sandy beach (minus the sea-foam, of course). Sprinkle the topping evenly all over the apple filling in the cast-iron skillet.

Next, place the cast-iron skillet in your preheated Big Green Egg and bake it for 30 minutes, or until the topping has browned and the apple juices are bubbling up through the topping. Remove the skillet from your Big Green Egg, let the apple crumble cool slightly and then serve it to your friends and family waiting on dessert!

CHAPTER 5

Can You Really Do That?

RECIPES TO HARNESS ALL THE ADD-ONS THE BIG GREEN EGG HAS TO OFFER

Part of the fun of being a Big Green Egg owner is all the extras and add-ons you can get to augment your cooking environment. In this chapter, I have recipes for some of my favorite EGGcessories that will help you get up to speed quickly. You are about to discover how crazy delicious—and fun!—food can be when you make them with tools like a wok, the EGGspander and cast-iron cookware on the Big Green Egg.

FEEDS: 8 people

APPROXIMATE COOK TIME: 2–2½ hours

BIG GREEN EGG SETUP: Indirect

SUGGESTED WOOD TYPE: Pecan wood chunks

TOOLS AND ACCESSORIES: EGGspander base, convEGGtor, 5-quart (4.8-L) cast-iron Dutch oven

CHILI

2 lb (908 g) 80/20 ground beef

2 tbsp (36 g) kosher salt, divided

2 tsp (4 g) ground black pepper, divided

2 tbsp (30 ml) olive oil

1 yellow onion, diced

6 cloves garlic, minced

1 poblano chile, diced

1 (6-oz [168-g]) can tomato paste

1 (28-oz [840-ml]) can crushed tomatoes

2 cups (480 ml) low-sodium beef broth

12 oz (360 ml) beer

2 tbsp (12 g) ground cumin

1 tsp fresh thyme leaves

1 tsp finely chopped fresh oregano

1 tsp cayenne

½ tsp ground cinnamon

¼ cup (24 g) ancho chili powder

The Buddha's EGGspanded Beef Chili

It doesn't happen often here in Florida, but sometimes the weather cools enough to make some chili! One of the best uses for the Big Green Egg EGGspander is over-the-top chili. This style of chili is so much fun—you smoke and cook the meat over the chili mix below, infusing smoke flavor into both the meat and the chili. You will have a blast making this recipe and, of course, eating it with your guests!

Set up your Big Green Egg for indirect grilling (as described on page 20) using the EGGspander base and either the convEGGtor or two half-moon ceramic inserts. Preheat the Big Green Egg to 350°F (177°C). Place a 5-quart (4.8-L) cast-iron Dutch oven on the bottom grill grate sitting underneath the elevated cooking grid to preheat. While the Big Green Egg and Dutch oven are preheating, it's time to prep the chili ingredients.

In a medium bowl, mix the ground beef with 1 tablespoon (18 g) of the salt and 1 teaspoon of the pepper. Form the beef into a ball, place the ball on a baking sheet and place the baking sheet in the refrigerator.

When the Big Green Egg and Dutch oven have preheated, add the olive oil to the Dutch oven. When the oil is hot, add the onion, garlic and poblano and cook them for 2 to 3 minutes, until the onion is translucent. Add the tomato paste, crushed tomatoes, beef broth, beer, cumin, thyme, oregano, cayenne, cinnamon and ancho chili powder. Mix the ingredients well to combine them and let the mixture simmer for 10 minutes. Next, remove the Dutch oven from the Big Green Egg so you can set it up for the next step.

Mix in three chunks of pecan wood with the lump charcoal and reduce the temperature of the Big Green Egg to 275°F (135°C). As strange as this may sound, top off the lit lump charcoal with some fresh lump charcoal. This will starve the fire of oxygen, thus reducing the temperature for you.

1 (15-oz [420-g]) can pinto beans, drained and rinsed

1 (15-oz [420-g]) can black beans, drained and rinsed

1 (15-oz [420-g]) can great northern beans, drained and rinsed

GARNISHES

Corn chips

Sour cream

Shredded sharp Cheddar cheese

½ red onion, diced

1 cup (16 g) minced fresh cilantro

When the Big Green Egg is stable at 275°F (135°C) and the smoke is light gray in color, place the EGGspander Multi-Level Rack in the Big Green Egg. Now place the Dutch oven directly underneath the top rack of the EGGspander. Take the ball of beef out of the refrigerator and place it directly over the Dutch oven. This will allow the smoky drippings to fall directly into the Dutch oven. Close the lid of the Big Green Egg and cook the chili mixture and beef until the internal temperature of the beef is 150°F (66°C)—typically, this will take 1½ to 2 hours.

When the meat is ready, remove it from the top rack and place it in the Dutch oven, breaking up the meat and combining it with the chili mixture thoroughly. Add the pinto beans, black beans and great northern beans to the Dutch oven and mix them into the chili. Cook the chili for 30 minutes or so, until the beans are warmed through.

Remove the chili from the Big Green Egg and serve with the array of garnishes.

FEEDS: 4–6 people

APPROXIMATE COOK TIME:
10 minutes

BIG GREEN EGG SETUP:
Direct

TOOLS AND ACCESSORIES:
EGGspander base, Big
Green Egg Half Moon
Cast Iron Plancha Griddle

CRAB CAKES

1 lb (454 g) lump crabmeat

1 egg

1 cup (108 g) plain breadcrumbs

1 tbsp (3 g) minced fresh chives

¼ cup (60 ml) mayonnaise

1 tbsp (15 ml) Dijon mustard

1 tbsp (15 ml) Worcestershire
sauce

½ tsp kosher salt

½ tsp ground black pepper

¼ cup (60 ml) cooking oil

2 tbsp (6 g) finely chopped
fresh chives

Lemon slices

REMOULADE

½ cup (120 ml) mayonnaise

1 tbsp (15 g) sweet pickle relish

1 tbsp (15 ml) grainy mustard

1 tbsp (15 ml) ketchup

1 tsp hot sauce

1 tsp horseradish

1 tsp Cajun seasoning

¼ tsp smoked paprika

1 clove garlic, minced

Crab Cakes on the Plancha

While I was growing up in the Washington, DC, area, my father would often take me to Maryland to eat my fair share of crab cakes. They were a tasty treat that I loved to share with my family. This recipe is one of my favorites to make during the summertime. You can serve them by themselves as an app or main course, or try placing one in a toasted hamburger bun for the ultimate crab cake sandwich. I love to use Dizzy Pig Bayou-ish Blackening Seasoning for the Cajun seasoning in this.

Make the crab cake mixture at least 2 hours before you plan to cook the crab cakes. Take the crabmeat out of the packaging and drain it, looking for any shells that may be in the meat. In a medium bowl, combine the crab meat with the egg, breadcrumbs and minced chives. Make sure you form an even mixture without lumps. Next, mix together the mayonnaise, Dijon mustard, Worcestershire sauce, salt and pepper in a small bowl, then fold that mixture into the crabmeat mixture. Cover the bowl with plastic wrap and place it in the fridge to chill for 2 hours. The longer the crab cake mixture sits in the fridge, the better your chances of making crab cakes that do not fall apart.

While the crab cake mixture is resting, make the remoulade. Mix together all of the ingredients for the remoulade in a medium bowl until they are well combined. Store the remoulade in the fridge until you are ready to serve the crab cakes.

After the crab cake mixture has chilled for 2 hours, set up your Big Green Egg for direct grilling (as described on page 18) and preheat it to 350°F (177°C). For this cook, you will want to use the EGGspander base with the Big Green Egg Half Moon Cast Iron Plancha Griddle placed on the bottom tier, flat side up. Let the Big Green Egg and plancha preheat while you form the crab cakes.

Make six equal balls of the crabmeat mixture, using approximately ½ cup (114 g) for each ball. Press down on each ball and gently form it into a patty shape. When the Big Green Egg and plancha have preheated, coat the plancha with the cooking oil, place the crab cakes on the plancha and cook them for 4 minutes, until the bottom of each crab cake is nicely brown and set. Flip the crab cakes and cook them for 4 minutes on the other side. When the bottom of each crab cake is browned and set, remove the crab cakes and let them cool for 3 minutes.

Serve the crab cakes with a drizzle of the remoulade, chopped chives and lemon slices.

FEEDS: 4 people

APPROXIMATE COOK TIME: 20 minutes

BIG GREEN EGG SETUP: Direct

TOOLS AND ACCESSORIES: EGGspander base, Big Green Egg Half Moon Cast Iron Plancha Griddle

SALMON

2 tsp (4 g) paprika

1 tsp garlic powder

1 tsp onion powder

1 tsp dried oregano

2 tsp (12 g) kosher salt

½ tsp ground black pepper

½ tsp cayenne

1 (1-lb [454-g]) skinless salmon fillet

2 tbsp (30 ml) cooking oil

1 lemon, cut into wedges

CHARRED PINEAPPLE SALSA

1 pineapple, peeled, cored and diced

2 tbsp (30 ml) olive oil

1 jalapeño, diced

1 red bell pepper, deseeded and diced

½ red onion, diced

Juice of 1 lime

¼ cup (4 g) coarsely chopped fresh cilantro

Kosher salt, to taste

Blackened Salmon Fillet with Charred Pineapple Salsa

Though I am surrounded by fresh Gulf Coast seafood in my hometown of Gulfport, Florida, I cannot forget about one of my favorite fish to cook—salmon. The charred pineapple salsa brings a fresh sweet and savory element to the blackened salmon. This easy recipe is a perfect summertime treat and will certainly please your friends and family. I've included a homemade blackening seasoning in this recipe, but if you have a favorite brand of blackening seasoning, you can use that instead (I love Dizzy Pig Bayou-ish Blackening Seasoning).

Set up your Big Green Egg for direct grilling (as described on page 18) using the EGGspander base and the Big Green Egg Half Moon Cast Iron Plancha Griddle, flat side up. Preheat the Big Green Egg to 450°F (232°C). While the Big Green Egg and plancha are preheating, begin preparing the salmon.

In a small bowl, mix together the paprika, garlic powder, onion powder, oregano, salt, pepper and cayenne, then apply the seasoning to both sides of the salmon fillet. When the Big Green Egg and plancha have preheated, add the cooking oil to the plancha and spread it around with your spatula so the entire surface of the plancha is coated in oil.

When the oil is shimmering and slightly smoky, place your seasoned fillet on the plancha. Cook the salmon for 4 minutes, then flip it and cook it for 4 minutes on the other side. When your fish measures 145°F (63°C) on an instant-read thermometer, pull the blackened fillet off the plancha. Let the salmon rest on a cutting board for 5 minutes.

While the salmon rests, toss the diced pineapple with the olive oil and cook the pineapple on the plancha for 4 minutes, until it is charred on all sides. In a medium bowl, mix the charred pineapple with the jalapeño, bell pepper, onion, lime juice and cilantro. Season the salsa with the salt.

Divide the salmon in four equal portions, and then top each portion with the charred pineapple salsa.

FEEDS: 4 people

APPROXIMATE COOK TIME: 10–15 minutes

BIG GREEN EGG SETUP: Direct

TOOLS AND ACCESSORIES: EGGspander base, Big Green Egg Half Moon Cast Iron Plancha Griddle

1 tbsp (15 ml) cooking oil

2 tbsp (28 g) unsalted butter, divided

1 yellow onion, thinly sliced

8 oz (224 g) white mushrooms, thinly sliced

1 tsp garlic powder

Kosher salt

Ground black pepper (ideally 16 mesh)

1½ lb (681 g) boneless rib eye steak, thinly sliced

2 tsp (10 ml) Worcestershire sauce

8 slices provolone cheese

4 (8" [20-cm]-long) soft Italian sandwich hoagie rolls, split lengthwise and toasted

Classic Steak and Cheese on the Plancha

I grew up in the Washington, DC, area eating steak and cheese sandwiches at my favorite local pizza shop. Everyone has their favorite way of making (or ordering) steak and cheese sandwiches. I like mine with grilled onions and mushrooms. This recipe makes it easy to customize the veggie toppings based on what you like. Using the Big Green Egg is an enjoyable way to make a classic steak and cheese sandwich. Have fun!

Set up your Big Green Egg for direct grilling (as described on page 18) using the EGGspander base and the Big Green Egg Half Moon Cast Iron Plancha Griddle, flat side up. Preheat the Big Green Egg to 450°F (232°C). While the Big Green Egg and plancha are preheating, gather and prep the ingredients.

When the Big Green Egg and plancha have preheated, add the cooking oil to the plancha and spread it around with your spatula so the entire surface of the plancha is coated in oil. When the oil is shimmering and slightly smoky, add 1 tablespoon (14 g) of the butter and let it melt. When the butter has melted, add the onion, mushrooms and garlic powder, and then season the vegetables with the salt and pepper and stir them well. Continue cooking the vegetables for 5 to 6 minutes, stirring them frequently, until the onion is translucent and the mushrooms are slightly browned. Remove the onion and mushrooms from the plancha and set them aside.

Put your thinly sliced rib eye in a large bowl and season the meat with salt, pepper and the Worcestershire sauce. Add the remaining 1 tablespoon (14 g) of butter to the plancha. When the butter is bubbly, transfer your seasoned steak to the plancha. Cook the steak for 4 to 6 minutes, until it is cooked through and browned. Add the onion and mushrooms to the cooked meat and combine everything thoroughly. Spread the combined meat, onion and mushrooms out to create a flat layer and place the provolone cheese on top. Shut the rEGGulator and Draft Door of your Big Green Egg, close the lid and let the cheese melt for 2 to 3 minutes. When the cheese has melted, load a hoagie roll with a scoop of the steak and cheese sandwich filling. Repeat this step with the other hoagie rolls.

FEEDS: 6 people

APPROXIMATE COOK TIME:
2 hours to marinate,
30 minutes to cook

BIG GREEN EGG SETUP:
Direct

TOOLS AND ACCESSORIES:
EGGspander base, Big
Green Egg Half Moon
Cast Iron Plancha Griddle

SKIRT STEAK

2 lb (908 g) skirt steak

10 cloves garlic, minced

¼ cup (60 ml) fresh lime juice

¼ cup (60 ml) clear tequila

¼ cup (60 ml) soy sauce

1 bunch fresh cilantro leaves and stems, coarsely chopped

1 jalapeño, deseeded and diced

1 serrano chile, deseeded and diced

1 tsp ground cumin

1 tsp chili powder

1 tsp onion powder

1 tsp kosher salt

1 tsp ground black pepper (ideally 16 mesh)

2 tbsp (30 ml) cooking oil, divided

Skirt Steak Fajitas on the Plancha

I love cooking with the Big Green Egg's cast-iron plancha, as it has many uses. Making fajitas is always a fun cook, and the delicious results make everyone happy. This marinade gives the skirt steak a unique flavor, thanks to the tequila.

Trim the skirt steak of extra fat and silver skin, then cut it into 4-inch (10-cm)-long sections. Make the marinade by mixing together the garlic, lime juice, tequila, soy sauce, cilantro, jalapeño, serrano, cumin, chili powder, onion powder, salt and pepper in a medium bowl. Combine the skirt steak and the marinade in a large ziplock bag, and then place the bag in the fridge to let the steak marinate for 2 hours.

Set up your Big Green Egg for direct grilling (as described on page 18) using the EGGspander base and the Big Green Egg Half Moon Cast Iron Plancha Griddle, flat side up. Preheat the Big Green Egg to 450°F (232°C).

When the Big Green Egg and plancha have preheated, add 1 tablespoon (15 ml) of the cooking oil to the plancha and spread it around with your spatula so the entire surface of the plancha is coated in oil. Take the skirt steak out of the marinade and place it on the preheated plancha. Cook the meat for 3 minutes, then flip it and cook it for 3 minutes on the other side. Transfer the steak to a cutting board and loosely cover the steak with foil.

(continued)

Skirt Steak Fajitas on the Plancha (continued)

FAJITAS

1 red bell pepper, deseeded and cut into ½" (1-cm)-thick strips

1 yellow bell pepper, deseeded and cut into ½" (1-cm)-thick

1 green bell pepper, deseeded and cut into ½" (1-cm)-thick strips

1 yellow onion, cut into ½" (1-cm)-thick slices

1 tbsp (15 ml) olive oil

1 tsp kosher salt

1 tsp ground black pepper

1 tsp garlic powder

12 (6" [15-cm]) flour tortillas, warmed

1 cup (224 g) guacamole

1 cup (248 g) pico de gallo

½ cup (120 ml) sour cream

1 cup (113 g) shredded Cheddar cheese

1 cup (16 g) coarsely chopped fresh cilantro

In a large bowl, toss together the red bell pepper, yellow bell pepper, green bell pepper, onion, olive oil, salt, pepper and garlic powder. Add the remaining 1 tablespoon (15 ml) of cooking oil to the plancha, then add the veggies. Cook the vegetables, stirring them frequently for 10 minutes, until they are nicely charred. Transfer the veggies to a serving platter.

Slice the skirt steak against the grain into ½-inch (1.3-cm) strips and lay the strips on top of the cooked vegetables. Serve the fajitas with the warm tortillas, guacamole, pico de gallo, sour cream, Cheddar cheese and cilantro.

FEEDS: 4 people

APPROXIMATE COOK TIME:
10 minutes

BIG GREEN EGG SETUP:
Direct

TOOLS AND ACCESSORIES:
EGGspander base, Big
Green Egg Half Moon
Cast Iron Plancha Griddle

BURGERS

1 lb (454 g) 80/20 ground beef

Kosher salt

Ground black pepper (ideally 16 mesh)

2 tbsp (30 ml) vegetable oil

4 slices American cheese

4 toasted potato rolls

TOPPING IDEAS

Iceberg lettuce

Sliced tomatoes

Pickles

Ketchup

Mustard

Plancha Smash Burgers

Who doesn't love a good smash burger? When Big Green Egg released their cast-iron plancha, I knew right away the first thing I was going to cook on it—smash burgers! This simple recipe will deliver perfect diner-style burgers every time.

Set up your Big Green Egg for direct grilling (as described on page 18) using the EGGspander base and the Big Green Egg Half Moon Cast Iron Plancha Griddle, flat side up. Preheat the Big Green Egg to 450°F (232°C). While the Big Green Egg and plancha are preheating, prep the burger ingredients.

Divide the ground beef into four 4-ounce (112-g) balls. Place the balls on a baking sheet and season all sides of the balls liberally with the salt and pepper. When the Big Green Egg and plancha have preheated, add the oil to the plancha and spread it around with your spatula so the entire surface of the plancha is covered in the oil.

Place the burger balls on the plancha, ensuring there is enough space between each ball to smash it down into a patty. Now, using a metal spatula, press down on each of the burger balls until they are 4 inches (10 cm) in diameter and ½ inch (1.3 cm) thick. Cook the burgers undisturbed for 1 to 2 minutes, until a deep brown crust starts to form on the bottom of the patties. Using your metal spatula, flip each patty over. Place a slice of the American cheese on each patty and cook them for 1 to 2 minutes, until the cheese has melted. Remove the smash burgers and place one on each of the toasted potato rolls. Add your favorite toppings to the burgers.

FEEDS: 4 people

APPROXIMATE COOK TIME: 30 minutes

BIG GREEN EGG SETUP: Direct

TOOLS AND ACCESSORIES: EGGspander base, Big Green Egg Half Moon Cast Iron Plancha Griddle, cast-iron grill press

MOJO SAUCE

4 tbsp (60 ml) olive oil

½ cup (8 g) finely chopped fresh cilantro

1 tsp finely grated orange zest

¼ cup (60 ml) fresh orange juice

¼ cup (60 ml) fresh lime juice

1 tbsp (6 g) finely chopped fresh mint leaves

4 cloves garlic, minced

1 tsp dried oregano

1 tsp ground cumin

1 tsp kosher salt

CUBAN SANDWICHES

8 oz (224 g) leftover pulled pork

1 loaf Cuban bread or crusty baguette, sliced in half lengthwise

3 tbsp (45 ml) yellow mustard

4 oz (112 g) ham, thinly sliced

6 oz (168 g) Swiss cheese, thinly sliced

1 cup (155 g) dill pickle chips

1–2 tbsp (14–28 g) butter, softened

Pressed Cuban Sandwich on the Plancha

Since moving to the Tampa area of Florida, I have become obsessed with Cuban sandwiches. Few people realize this style of pressed sandwich actually did not originate in Cuba but rather in Tampa, Florida. This recipe for a Cuban sandwich is a great way to repurpose leftover pork, such as the Bone-In Pork Shoulder (page 38)!

Start by making the mojo sauce. Place all of the ingredients in a medium saucepan and heat them over medium heat until you see the mixture start to boil. Turn the heat to medium-low and simmer the mixture for 20 minutes, until the sauce is fragrant and starting to reduce. Using an immersion blender or a food processor, blend the mojo sauce to form a smooth paste. Allow this sauce to cool, then mix it with the leftover pulled pork. Set the mojo pork aside.

Set up your Big Green Egg for direct grilling (as described on page 18) using the EGGspander base and the Big Green Egg Half Moon Cast Iron Plancha Griddle, ribbed side up. Preheat the Big Green Egg to 350°F (177°C). While the Big Green Egg and plancha are preheating, assemble the sandwiches.

Slice the Cuban bread into four equal portions to create four sandwiches, then divide the mojo pork into four equal portions. Spread a layer of mustard on each side of the cut bread, then layer on the mojo pork, ham, Swiss cheese and pickle chips. Top the layered filling with the other half of the sliced bread to create the sandwiches.

Spread about half of the butter on the bottom of the bread, then gently place one of the sandwiches, buttered side down, on the preheated cast-iron plancha. Using a cast-iron grill press, firmly press down on the sandwich and leave the grill press on top of the sandwich. After 3 minutes, remove the grill press and apply the remaining half of the butter to the top of the bread. Flip the sandwich over so the buttered top is now in contact with the plancha. Using the sandwich press, firmly press down on the sandwich and cook it for 3 minutes, until the bread is nicely toasted and the cheese is melty. Repeat this process with the remaining sandwiches.

Slice the sandwiches in half and enjoy a taste of my hometown!

FEEDS: 4 people

APPROXIMATE COOK TIME:
20 minutes

BIG GREEN EGG SETUP:
Direct

TOOLS AND ACCESSORIES:
EGGspander base, Big
Green Egg Half Moon
Cast Iron Plancha Griddle

LIME CREMA

Zest and juice of 1 lime

8 oz (240 ml) sour cream

1 clove garlic, minced

¼ tsp kosher salt

PORK BURRITOS

2 tbsp (30 ml) olive oil,
divided

½ red onion, diced

1 jalapeño, deseeded and
diced

2 cloves garlic, minced

8 oz (224 g) leftover pulled
pork

1 cup (186 g) cooked white
rice

8 oz (224 g) black beans,
drained and rinsed

¼ cup (60 ml) your favorite
BBQ sauce

1 tbsp (15 ml) fresh lime juice

½ cup (8 g) chopped cilantro

4 (10" [25-cm]) flour tortillas

¼ cup (28 g) shredded
Cheddar cheese

¼ cup (28 g) shredded
Monterey Jack cheese

Pulled Pork Burritos with Lime Crema

If you have leftover pulled pork from smoking a Boston butt—such as from the Hot and Fast Pulled Pork (a.k.a. Turbo Butt) on page 72—this recipe is for you. Crunchy, savory and deeply satisfying, this pulled pork burrito is so good. The complementary flavor of the crema makes this dish one to remember.

Set up your Big Green Egg for direct grilling (as described on page 18) using the EGGspander base and the Big Green Egg Half Moon Cast Iron Plancha Griddle, flat side up. Preheat the Big Green Egg to 350°F (177°C). While the Big Green Egg and plancha are preheating, make the lime crema.

In a small bowl, stir together all of the ingredients for the lime crema. When the ingredients are well combined, cover the bowl and place it in the fridge until you are ready to serve the burritos.

When the Big Green Egg and plancha have preheated, add 1 tablespoon (15 ml) of the olive oil to the plancha and spread it around with your spatula so the entire surface of the plancha is coated in oil. When the oil is shimmering and slightly smoky, place the onion, jalapeño and garlic on the plancha and cook the vegetables for 5 to 6 minutes, stirring them constantly, until the onion is translucent and the jalapeño has browned. Next, add the pulled pork, rice and beans. Mix the ingredients together well and cook them for 2 to 4 minutes, until the mixture has warmed through. Add the BBQ sauce, lime juice and cilantro and mix them together well with the other ingredients. Transfer the burrito filling to a medium bowl, and then get your tortillas ready.

Warm the tortillas in the microwave for 30 seconds to make them more pliable. Now, put some of the pork filling in the center of a tortilla, add some of the Cheddar cheese and Monterey Jack cheese. Fold the bottom edge of the tortilla to meet the filling, and then pull the tortilla's sides over so that they are covering each another. Roll the burrito up tightly and set it aside. Repeat this process with the remaining tortillas and filling.

Pour the remaining 1 tablespoon (15 ml) of olive oil on the plancha. When the oil is shimmering and smoking slightly, place the burritos seam side down on the plancha. Cook them for 1 to 2 minutes per side, until the tortillas are nicely browned and slightly crunchy.

Serve the burritos with a drizzle of the lime crema.

FEEDS: 2–4 people

APPROXIMATE COOK TIME:
40 minutes

BIG GREEN EGG SETUP:
Indirect and direct

TOOLS AND ACCESSORIES:
EGGspander base and top,
convEGGtor,

1 (2-lb [908-g]) porterhouse
steak

1 tsp olive oil

1 tbsp (12 g) Big Green
Egg Classic Steakhouse
Seasoning or steak seasoning
of your choice

Reverse–Seared Porterhouse Steak with Cowboy Finish

The five-piece EGGspander has so many uses it is hard to cover them all in one book. By far, one of the cleverest design elements of the EGGspander top is that it gives you the ability to cook cowboy-style. The reason this method is called "cowboy cooking" is because it is akin to the way cowboys cook their meals over a live fire while they are out on the range. Cooking directly in the coals or on a grill grate that sits directly on top of the coals is what defines cowboy-style. Thankfully, the two-piece EGGspander Multi-Level Rack turns upside down, allowing you to cook right on the coals with little to no fuss. This porterhouse steak is a simple, delicious and practically foolproof way to try out the cowboy cooking method.

Set up your Big Green Egg for indirect grilling (as described on page 20) using the EGGspander base and the convEGGtor or two half-moon ceramic inserts. Preheat the Big Green Egg to 250°F (121°C). While the Big Green Egg is preheating, prep the steak for this cook.

Take the steak out of its packaging and rub it with the olive oil. Next, season the steak liberally all over with the Big Green Egg Classic Steakhouse Seasoning. (This is Big Green Egg's version of Montreal steak seasoning—if you don't have the Big Green Egg brand, any type of similar steak rub will do.) Let the steak sit at room temperature until the Big Green Egg is at temperature.

When the Big Green Egg is ready, place the steak on the grill grate and cook it for 15 minutes. Flip the steak and cook it for 15 minutes on the other side, or until the internal temperature reaches 115°F (46°C). Pull the steak from the Big Green Egg and let it rest while you set up your EGGspander for the big cowboy finish.

Using heat-resistant gloves to protect your hands, remove the EGGspander base and associated ceramic inserts. Here comes the fun part: Configure the EGGspander's two-piece Multi-Level Rack to sit upside down in your Big Green Egg. The top part of the EGGspander, when turned upside down, will sit nicely on top of the Fire Ring, placing the grill grate directly over the lit lump charcoal below. Open the Draft Door all the way and the rEGGulator three-fourths of the way to allow the lump charcoal to rise in temperature. When the temperature of your Big Green Egg is 500°F (260°C), it's time to get that cowboy sear.

Make sure to wear heat-resistant gloves for this portion of the cook to protect your hands. Take the rested porterhouse and place it on the grill grate, which is sitting directly above the flaming charcoal below. Cook the steak for 1 minute, then flip it and cook it for 1 minute on the other side. When you have a beautiful dark crust on your steak, remove it from the Big Green Egg and serve it.

FEEDS: 4 people

APPROXIMATE COOK TIME:
Overnight to marinate, 20
minutes to cook

BIG GREEN EGG SETUP:
Direct

TOOLS AND ACCESSORIES:
EGGspander base, carbon-
steel wok

2 tbsp (30 ml) rice wine
vinegar, divided

2 tbsp (30 ml) soy sauce,
divided

1 tbsp (15 ml) toasted sesame
oil

2 tbsp (36 g) gochujang paste,
divided

3 tbsp (51 g) white miso paste

Zest of 1 lemon

2 tbsp (30 g) minced fresh
ginger

6 cloves garlic, minced

2 lb (908 g) boneless, skinless
chicken thighs

Korean–Style Chicken and Asparagus Stir–Fry

Once you start cooking with your carbon-steel wok, you will want to do it again and again. This recipe takes some preparation, as the meat needs to marinate overnight. However, it is well worth the wait—the deep umami flavor of this marinade is so darn good. You can substitute the soba noodles with cooked white rice if you prefer.

The day before you plan to cook the dish, you need to marinate the chicken. To make the marinade, combine 1 tablespoon (15 ml) of the rice wine vinegar, 1 tablespoon (15 ml) of the soy sauce, sesame oil, 1 tablespoon (18 g) of the gochujang, white miso, lemon zest, ginger and garlic in a food processor. Process the ingredients until they form a thick paste. Set this paste aside.

Trim the chicken thighs of excess fat and sinew, then cut them into 1-inch (2.5-cm) chunks. In a large ziplock bag or lidded bowl, mix the chicken with the marinade paste and refrigerate the chicken overnight.

The next day, set up your Big Green Egg for direct grilling (as described on page 18) using the EGGspander base and the carbon-steel wok. Preheat the Big Green Egg and wok to 450°F (232°C). Make sure to wear a heat-resistant glove for this cook to protect your cooking hand while over the live fire. When your Big Green Egg has preheated, close the Draft Door all the way, as you will be cooking with the lid open. Closing the Draft Door will help reduce the amount of air coming into the Fire Box, giving you better temperature control while you are cooking. As the Big Green Egg preheats, prep the remaining stir-fry ingredients.

In a small bowl, combine the remaining 1 tablespoon (15 ml) of rice wine vinegar, 1 tablespoon (15 ml) of soy sauce and 1 tablespoon (18 g) of gochujang to make the stir-fry sauce. Remove the marinated chicken from the fridge.

4 tbsp (60 ml) peanut oil, divided

1 yellow onion, thinly sliced

1 bunch asparagus, cut into 2″ (5-cm) pieces

1 bundle soba noodles, cooked

4 scallions, green parts thinly sliced and white parts discarded

2 tbsp (18 g) toasted sesame seeds

Heat 2 tablespoons (30 ml) of the peanut oil in the carbon-steel wok. When the oil is smoking slightly, it is time to start cooking. First, add the chicken and cook it for 8 to 10 minutes, stirring it frequently. When the chicken is nicely browned, remove it from the wok and set it to the side. Next, add the remaining 2 tablespoons (30 ml) of peanut oil to the wok, then add the onion and asparagus. Sauté the vegetables for 4 to 5 minutes, stirring them frequently, until the onion is translucent and the asparagus is nicely browned. At this point, return the chicken to the wok and stir it with the vegetables until everything is well combined. Add the stir-fry sauce and soba noodles. Mix the ingredients together well and cook them for 2 minutes, stirring them constantly.

Serve the stir-fry in bowls, with each serving topped with the scallions and sesame seeds.

FEEDS: 4 people

APPROXIMATE COOK TIME:
20 minutes

BIG GREEN EGG SETUP:
Direct

TOOLS AND ACCESSORIES:
EGGspander base,
carbon-steel wok

STIR-FRY SAUCE

3 tbsp (45 ml) reduced-sodium soy sauce

2 tbsp (30 ml) oyster sauce

1 tbsp (15 ml) rice wine vinegar

1 tbsp (14 g) packed brown sugar

1 tbsp (15 g) grated fresh ginger

4 cloves garlic, minced

1 tsp toasted sesame oil

1 tsp cornstarch

1 tsp chili-garlic sauce

SHRIMP AND SNOW PEA STIR-FRY

2 tbsp (30 ml) peanut oil

½ white onion, thinly sliced

6 oz (168 g) snow peas, strings removed, washed and dried

4 carrots, diced

1½ lb (681 g) medium shrimp, peeled and deveined

1 bundle soba noodles, cooked

4 scallions, thinly sliced

1 tbsp (9 g) toasted sesame seeds

Shrimp and Snow Pea Stir–Fry

The live-fire environment of the Big Green Egg is a great way to make delicious food with your wok. This recipe is one of my favorites to make for my wife on any given weeknight. I hope you enjoy it as much as she does!

Set up your Big Green Egg for direct grilling (as described on page 18) using the EGGspander base and the carbon-steel wok. Preheat the Big Green Egg to 450°F (232°C). Make sure to wear a heat-resistant glove for this cook to protect your cooking hand while over the live fire. When your Big Green Egg has preheated, close the Draft Door all the way, as you will be cooking with the lid open. Closing the Draft Door will help reduce the amount of air coming into the Fire Box, giving you better temperature control while you are cooking. As the Big Green Egg preheats, prep the stir-fry ingredients.

To make the stir-fry sauce, mix together the soy sauce, oyster sauce, rice wine vinegar, brown sugar, ginger, garlic, sesame oil, cornstarch and chili-garlic sauce in a small bowl. Set the stir-fry sauce aside.

Heat the peanut oil in the hot carbon-steel wok. When the oil is smoking slightly, it is time to start cooking. Add the onion, snow peas and carrots and stir-fry them for 5 minutes, until the snow peas and carrots are bright in color and the onion is translucent. Next, add the shrimp and stir-fry the mixture for 5 to 6 minutes, until the shrimp are opaque and slightly curled. Finally, add the stir-fry sauce and stir-fry the ingredients for 8 to 10 minutes, until the sauce is slightly thick and evenly mixed with the vegetables and shrimp.

Remove the wok from the Big Green Egg and let the stir-fry cool for 5 minutes before serving it over the soba noodles. Garnish each serving with the scallions and sesame seeds.

FEEDS: 4 people

APPROXIMATE COOK TIME: 15 minutes

BIG GREEN EGG SETUP: Direct

TOOLS AND ACCESSORIES: EGGspander base, carbon-steel wok

STIR-FRY SAUCE

¼ cup (60 ml) soy sauce

2 tsp (6 g) cornstarch

1 tbsp (14 g) brown sugar

1 tbsp (15 g) minced fresh ginger

BEEF STIR-FRY

1½ lb (681 g) flank steak, thinly sliced

1 tbsp (15 ml) peanut oil

2 cups (182 g) broccoli florets

¼ cup (60 ml) beef broth

4 cloves garlic, minced

2 tsp (10 ml) toasted sesame oil

Kosher salt

Ground black pepper (ideally 16 mesh)

Cooked white rice

2 tbsp (18 g) toasted sesame seeds

4 scallions, green parts thinly sliced and white parts discarded

Classic Beef and Broccoli Stir-Fry

If you want to master wok cooking on the Big Green Egg, you need to have a good beef and broccoli stir-fry under your belt. This classic dish always delivers, as it is quick, easy and packed with flavor. Once you have mastered this recipe, you can feel confident about tackling more involved wok recipes. But my guess is you will make this one over and over again!

Set up your Big Green Egg for direct grilling (as described on page 18) using the EGGspander base and the carbon-steel wok. Preheat the Big Green Egg to 450°F (232°C). Make sure to wear heat-resistant gloves for this cook to protect your cooking hand while it is over the live fire. In addition, when your Big Green Egg has preheated, close the Draft Door all the way, as you will be cooking with the lid open. Closing the Draft Door will help reduce the amount of air coming into the Fire Box, giving you better temperature control while cooking. As the Big Green Egg preheats, prep the stir-fry ingredients.

In a large bowl, combine the soy sauce, cornstarch, brown sugar and ginger. Add the steak to the stir-fry sauce, ensuring it is coated in the sauce. Set the bowl of steak and stir-fry sauce aside.

Heat the peanut oil in the carbon-steel wok. When the oil is smoking slightly, it is time to start cooking. Add the steak to the wok and cook it for 4 to 6 minutes, stirring it constantly, until it is well browned. Remove the meat from the wok and set it aside. Next, add the broccoli and stir-fry it for 1 to 2 minutes, until it is lightly browned. Add the beef broth, cover the wok with aluminum foil and allow the broccoli to steam in the broth for 2 to 3 minutes. Remove the foil and add the garlic and sesame oil. Continue cooking and stirring the broccoli for 1 minute to allow the garlic to become fragrant. Add the beef back to the wok, season with salt and pepper and mix the ingredients together well.

Serve the beef and broccoli stir-fry over the rice and topped with the sesame seeds and scallions.

FEEDS: 4–6 people

APPROXIMATE COOK TIME:
3 hours

BIG GREEN EGG SETUP:
Indirect and direct

SUGGESTED WOOD TYPE:
Apple or pecan chunks

TOOLS AND ACCESSORIES:
convEGGtor, EGGspander
base, carbon-steel wok

6 lb (2.7 kg) bone-in, skin-on
chicken pieces (drumsticks
and thighs)

2 tbsp (36 g) kosher salt,
divided

2 tsp (4 g) ground black
pepper (ideally 16 mesh),
divided

2 eggs

1½ cups (360 ml) buttermilk

5 cups (1.2 L) vegetable oil

1½ cups (188 g) all-purpose
flour

1 tbsp (7 g) paprika

1 tsp garlic powder

Wok and Roll Fried Chicken

This isn't your grandmother's fried chicken recipe! This recipe harnesses the power of the Big Green Egg in two different ways: smoking and frying. While this dish has many moving parts, it is totally worth the effort, delivering smoky fried chicken that is beyond description.

Set up your Big Green Egg for indirect grilling (as described on page 20) using the convEGGtor. Add two or three chunks of apple or pecan wood to the lump charcoal to get some smoke flavor on the chicken. Preheat your Big Green Egg to 225°F (107°C).

Season the chicken pieces with 1 tablespoon (18 g) salt and 1 teaspoon pepper. When the Big Green Egg's temperature is stable and the smoke is gray in color, place the chicken in the Big Green Egg. Smoke the chicken for 2 hours, or until the internal temperature of the chicken reaches 155°F (68°C).

Remove the chicken from the Big Green Egg. In a large bowl, mix together the eggs and buttermilk, then add the smoked chicken. Soak the chicken in the buttermilk mixture for 30 minutes.

Now set up the Big Green Egg for direct grilling (as described on page 18) using the EGGspander base and the carbon-steel wok. Carefully fill the wok with the vegetable oil, making sure the oil is well below the edges of the wok. You want just enough oil in the wok to cover the chicken but not enough to spill over and catch fire. Preheat the Big Green Egg to 400°F (204°C), close the lid and let the oil come up to 350°F (177°C).

While the Big Green Egg is preheating, prep the chicken for frying. In a medium bowl, mix together the flour, remaining 1 tablespoon (18 g) salt, remaining 1 teaspoon pepper, paprika and garlic powder, and then transfer the flour mixture to a large ziplock bag. When the Big Green Egg and the oil have preheated, remove the chicken from the buttermilk mixture and place a few chicken pieces in the bag containing the seasoned flour mixture. Close the bag and shake it to coat the chicken in the flour. Fry the chicken, two or three pieces at a time, in the preheated oil for 6 to 8 minutes, until the chicken is golden brown and crispy and its internal temperature is 165°F (74°C). Remove the chicken with a slotted spoon and place it on a baking sheet lined with paper towels. Continue frying the chicken in batches until all of the chicken is cooked. Allow the chicken to cool slightly, then serve.

FEEDS: 4 to 6 people

APPROXIMATE COOK TIME:
3 hours

BIG GREEN EGG SETUP:
Indirect and direct

SUGGESTED WOOD TYPE:
Apple or hickory chunks

TOOLS AND ACCESSORIES:
convEGGtor, wire baking
rack, EGGspander base,
carbon-steel wok

RIBS

2 racks baby back ribs

2 tsp (12 g) kosher salt

2 tsp (4 g) ground black
pepper (ideally 16 mesh)

2 tsp (6 g) garlic powder

1 tbsp (15 ml) hot sauce

4 cups (960 ml) vegetable oil

3 cups (375 g) all-purpose
flour

4 scallions, green parts
thinly sliced and white parts
discarded

2 tbsp (18 g) toasted sesame
seeds

General Tso's Smofried Ribs

Smoked-then-fried ribs? You read that right! This dish combines both techniques and reaps the benefits. Tossed with a delicious General Tso–inspired sauce, these ribs are not only fun to make but fun to eat too. Your friends and family will be wowed by this dish.

Set up your Big Green Egg for indirect grilling (as described on page 20) using the convEGGtor or two half-moon ceramic inserts. Add three chunks of apple or hickory to the lump charcoal (as described on page 16) for some smoky flavor on the ribs. Preheat your Big Green Egg to 275°F (135°C). While the Big Green Egg is preheating, prepare your ribs.

Pull the membrane from the back of the ribs and slice the racks into single ribs. In a small bowl, mix together the salt, pepper and garlic powder. In a large bowl, toss the ribs with the hot sauce and seasoning mixture until they are evenly coated. Place your ribs on a wire baking rack.

When the Big Green Egg has preheated and the smoke is light gray in color, place the ribs—still on the wire baking rack—inside the Big Green Egg and smoke them for 2 hours, flipping the ribs over halfway through the cook. Remove the ribs from the Big Green Egg and cover them with aluminum foil.

Wear heat-resistant gloves to remove the convEGGtor from the Big Green Egg, so that your Big Green Egg is now set up for direct grilling. With the EGGspander base in place, add your carbon-steel wok to the Big Green Egg. Bump the heat up to 350°F (177°C) and carefully fill the wok with the vegetable oil, making sure the oil is well below the edges of the wok. You want just enough oil in the wok to cover the ribs but not enough to spill over and catch fire. Let the oil and wok preheat.

Place the flour in a large bowl and, working in batches, dredge your cooked ribs in the flour. Brush excess flour from the ribs, and then wait for the oil to reach 350°F (177°C). When the oil is ready, fry the ribs in small batches for 3 to 4 minutes per batch, until they are golden brown and crunchy. When each batch is done, remove the ribs from the wok and set them on a baking sheet lined with paper towels to absorb excess oil.

(continued)

General Tso's Smofried Ribs (continued)

GENERAL TSO'S SAUCE

4 tbsp (60 g) sugar

3 tbsp (45 ml) low-sodium chicken stock

3 tbsp (45 ml) soy sauce

2 tbsp (30 ml) sherry cooking wine

2 tbsp (30 ml) rice wine vinegar

1 tbsp (9 g) cornstarch

1 tsp toasted sesame oil

2 tsp (10 ml) peanut oil

2 cloves garlic, minced

1" (2.5-cm) piece fresh ginger, minced

2 tsp (4 g) red pepper flakes

2 scallions, green parts minced and white parts discarded

8 scallions, white parts cut into 1" (2.5-cm) pieces and green parts discarded

Before moving on, note that you can make the General Tso's sauce on your stove if you prefer not to mess with disposing of the hot cooking oil. In that case, you can allow the oil to cool and then dispose of it. If, after all the ribs are fried, you want to make the sauce on the Big Green Egg, carefully remove the oil from the wok by draining it into a large metal can or other heat-resistant vessel.

Place the wok back on the Big Green Egg and preheat it to 350°F (177°C) to make the sauce. While the wok is preheating, mix together the sugar, chicken stock, soy sauce, sherry, rice wine vinegar, cornstarch and sesame oil in a small bowl. Stir the mixture until all of the cornstarch has dissolved. Set the mixture aside.

When the wok is preheated, add the peanut oil, garlic, ginger, red pepper flakes and minced scallions. Cook the aromatics for 2 to 3 minutes, stirring them constantly, until the mixture is fragrant and the garlic and ginger are soft. Now stir in the sauce mixture and combine it with the aromatics. Cook the mixture for 1 to 2 minutes, stirring it frequently, until it is gently boiling and the sauce is starting to thicken. Add the white parts of the scallions and stir the ingredients together.

Now add the smofried ribs to the sauce and toss them with the sauce to coat them evenly. Remove the ribs from the Big Green Egg and serve them garnished with the sliced scallions and sesame seeds.

FEEDS: 6–8 people

APPROXIMATE COOK TIME:
8 hours to prep meat,
2–3 hours to cook

BIG GREEN EGG SETUP:
Indirect

TOOLS AND ACCESSORIES:
EGGspander base and top,
convEGGtor, temperature
control unit

2 lb (908 g) London broil beef

1 cup (220 g) dark brown sugar

¾ cup (180 ml) soy sauce

3 tbsp (45 ml) Worcestershire sauce

1 tbsp (7 g) smoked paprika

1 tsp ground black pepper (ideally 16 mesh)

1 tsp red pepper flakes

1 tsp onion powder

½ tsp garlic powder

Beef Jerky

This is a classic beef jerky recipe that is finger-licking delicious. What I like about using the EGGspander for this cook is that you can take advantage of the vertical space higher in the Big Green Egg's dome to double your meat output. You will find yourself making this multiple times for the perfect on-the-go snack.

Trim the London broil of any excess fat and sinew. Place the meat in a large ziplock plastic bag, and then place the bag in the freezer for 2 hours to allow the meat to tighten up but not freeze. Remove the meat from the freezer and slice it as thinly as you can, following the grain of the meat, into long strips.

In a medium bowl, mix the brown sugar, soy sauce, Worcestershire sauce, paprika, black pepper, red pepper flakes, onion powder and garlic powder. Combine the meat and marinade in a large ziplock bag, and let the meat marinate in the refrigerator for 6 hours.

Set up your Big Green Egg for indirect grilling (as described on page 20) using the EGGspander base and the elevated sliding cooking grid. Preheat the Big Green Egg to 175°F (79°C). (I strongly recommend using a temperature control unit for this cook, such as the EGG Genius or Flame Boss 500-WiFi Kamado Smoker Controller Kit.) While the Big Green Egg is preheating, it's time to prep the meat for this cook.

Take the meat out of the marinade and dry it off with paper towels. When the Big Green Egg has preheated and the temperature is steady, gently lay the thin strips of meat on the bottom grill grate and then on the top grill grate, so that you have two single layers of meat ready to cook. Let the beef slices cook like this for 2 to 3 hours. You can start checking the meat in your Big Green Egg after the first hour to see how it's coming along—you want the jerky to be somewhat stiff but able to bend without breaking. Remove the jerky when it is finished and let it cool in an open container. Once the jerky has completely cooled, store it in an airtight container in the fridge for 1 to 2 months.

CHAPTER 6

Get the Party Started

GO-TO APPETIZER RECIPES FOR EVERY EVENT

If you are a Big Green Egg owner, chances are you like to host! This chapter has some of my favorite appetizer and starter recipes to help get your next event going in style. The recipes in this chapter deliver each and every time. And what's more, they are so good, you may just make several and skip the main course!

FEEDS: 6 people

APPROXIMATE COOK TIME: 20 minutes

BIG GREEN EGG SETUP: Indirect

TOOLS AND ACCESSORIES: convEGGtor, wire baking rack

6 oz (168 g) goat cheese, softened

20 medjool dates, pits removed

10 slices bacon, halved

⅓ cup (80 ml) hot honey

1 tbsp (3 g) finely chopped fresh chives

Hot Honey–Glazed Bacon–Wrapped Dates

This is one of my go-to appetizers when my wife and I are hosting at home. This quick and easy dish satisfies everyone who takes a bite. You will find yourself hosting a party just for an excuse to make this again.

Set up your Big Green Egg for indirect grilling (as described on page 20) using the convEGGtor. Preheat the Big Green Egg to 400°F (204°C). While the Big Green Egg is preheating, start assembling the stuffed dates.

Place the softened goat cheese in a small ziplock bag and cut a small piece from of the corner of the bag with scissors. Using the bag, pipe the goat cheese into each of the dates. Wrap each of the stuffed dates with a piece of bacon, securing the bacon with a toothpick to hold it in place. Brush each of the dates with the hot honey.

Coat a wire baking rack with cooking spray and lay the dates evenly across the wire rack. When your Big Green Egg has preheated, place the wire rack inside and let the dates cook for 15 to 20 minutes. When the bacon has rendered and is nicely browned, remove the wire rack and let the dates cool for 5 minutes before garnishing them with the chives.

FEEDS: 6 to 8 people

APPROXIMATE COOK TIME: 30 minutes

BIG GREEN EGG SETUP: Indirect

TOOLS AND ACCESSORIES: convEGGtor, 12" (30-cm) cast-iron skillet

2 tbsp (30 ml) olive oil

1 lb (454 g) Snake River Farms American Wagyu ground beef

1 yellow onion, diced

2 cloves garlic, minced

2 tbsp (24 g) Dizzy Pig Fajita-ish Mexican Seasoning

2 (10-oz [280-g]) cans RoTel®

1 (16-oz [454-g]) block Velveeta®, cubed

1 cup (112 g) shredded Monterey Jack cheese

Tortilla chips

2 tbsp (2 g) coarsely chopped fresh cilantro leaves

The Ultimate Queso Dip

When you take your first bit of this dip, you will know why I named it what I did. If you do not have American Wagyu ground beef, you can substitute 80/20 ground beef. But trust me, it is worth the effort to find the gourmet upgrade. Game day will never be the same!

Set up your Big Green Egg for indirect grilling (as described on page 20) using the convEGGtor. Preheat the Big Green Egg to 400°F (204°C). Place a 12-inch (30-cm) cast-iron skillet in the Big Green Egg to preheat. While the Big Green Egg and skillet are preheating, assemble your ingredients.

Note: Make sure to wear heat-resistant gloves to protect your hands while cooking this recipe.

When the Big Green Egg and skillet are heated, open the Big Green Egg's lid and close the Draft Door to prevent the charcoal from getting too hot. Add the oil to the skillet, then the ground beef. Cook the beef for 5 to 8 minutes, stirring it and breaking it up, so that it browns and cooks evenly. When the beef is cooked through and nicely browned, transfer it to a medium bowl and set it aside. Add the onion and garlic to the skillet and cook them for 2 to 3 minutes, until the onion is translucent and the garlic is fragrant. Next, add the Dizzy Pig Fajita-ish Seasoning and RoTel and mix the ingredients together well.

Start adding the Velveeta a couple of cubes at a time, folding them into the veggie mixture as they melt. Continue to do this for about 5 minutes, until all of the Velveeta has been added and has melted. Now do the same thing with the Monterey Jack cheese, adding a small handful at a time and stirring to combine it with the Velveeta and RoTel mixture—this should take about 5 minutes. When all the cheese has been added and is nicely melted, remove the skillet from the Big Green Egg and fold in the ground beef.

Serve the queso with chips and garnish it with the cilantro.

FEEDS: 4 people

APPROXIMATE COOK TIME:
8–10 minutes

BIG GREEN EGG SETUP:
Indirect

TOOLS AND ACCESSORIES:
convEGGtor, muffin pan

1 lb (454 g) leftover pulled pork, coarsely chopped

2 cups (480 ml) your favorite BBQ sauce

3 tbsp (42 g) butter, softened

12 canned biscuits

2 cups (226 g) shredded sharp Cheddar cheese

3 scallions, thinly sliced

Gran Judy's BBQ Cups

This recipe was inspired by my mother-in-law, Judy Buckman (a.k.a. Gran Judy). The original dish uses ground beef and canned sauce; my version uses leftover pulled pork (such as the Bone-In Pork Shoulder on page 38) and BBQ sauce. This dish is something we made often for our son while he was in high school. You will find yourself going to this recipe time and time again to satisfy the hungry mouths in your family.

Set up your Big Green Egg for indirect grilling (as described on page 20) using the convEGGtor. Preheat the Big Green Egg to 400°F (204°C).

While your Big Green Egg is preheating, mix the leftover pulled pork with the BBQ sauce in a large bowl.

Rub each well of a muffin pan with the butter to grease the pan. Next, flatten each biscuit and push it into the bottom and sides of a well of the muffin pan. Fill the biscuit cups about one-third full of the pulled pork mixture and top the pork with the Cheddar cheese.

When the Big Green Egg has preheated, place the muffin pan inside and bake the BBQ cups for 8 to 10 minutes, until the biscuits are nicely browned and the cheese has melted. Remove the muffin pan from the Big Green Egg and allow it to cool for 5 minutes. Remove the BBQ cups from the muffin pan and top them with the scallions.

FEEDS: 8–12 people

APPROXIMATE COOK TIME:
45 minutes

BIG GREEN EGG SETUP:
Indirect

TOOLS AND ACCESSORIES:
convEGGtor, wire baking
rack

8 oz (224 g) goat cheese,
softened

1 tbsp (12 g) your favorite
BBQ rub

1 cup (113 g) shredded sharp
Cheddar cheese

12 jalapeños, deseeded and
cut in half lengthwise

12 medium shrimp, peeled
and deveined

12 oz (336 g) bacon, thinly
sliced

1 tbsp (3 g) finely chopped
fresh parsley

Shrimp Atomic Buffalo Treats

If there is one staple you find at any EGGfest across the country, it is an Atomic Buffalo Turd. This is a version of jalapeño poppers that is always a crowd-pleaser. I wanted to upscale my version of this classic by substituting shrimp for the cocktail sausages and goat cheese for the cream cheese. This recipe might sound strange at first, but after your first bite, you will be a convert.

Set up your Big Green Egg for indirect grilling (as described on page 20) using the convEGGtor. Preheat the Big Green Egg to 350°F (177°C). While the Big Green Egg is preheating, start assembling the stuffed jalapeños.

In a medium bowl, mix the goat cheese with the BBQ rub and Cheddar cheese. Using a teaspoon, spoon the goat cheese mixture into each of the jalapeño halves. Now cut the shrimp so they lay flat like tempura-style shrimp. To do this, you need to make a few shallow slits in the belly of the shrimp. This will release the tension, allowing the shrimp to straighten and lay flat. Place the flattened shrimp in the stuffed jalapeños. Wrap each stuffed jalapeño with a piece of bacon, then secure the bacon with a toothpick to hold it in place.

Coat a wire baking rack with cooking spray and lay the bacon-wrapped stuffed jalapeños evenly across the wire rack. When your Big Green Egg has preheated, place the wire rack inside and let the stuffed jalapeños cook for 45 minutes. When the bacon has rendered and is nicely browned, remove the wire rack and let the stuffed jalapeños cool for 5 minutes before garnishing them with the parsley.

SERVES: 4–8 people

APPROXIMATE COOK TIME: 45 minutes

BIG GREEN EGG SETUP: Direct

TOOLS AND ACCESSORIES: EGGspander base, Big Green Egg Half Moon Cast Iron Plancha Griddle

HONEY–CHIPOTLE SAUCE

2 tsp (10 ml) olive oil

½ yellow onion, diced

2 cloves garlic, minced

1½ cups (360 ml) ketchup

1 (12-oz [336-g]) can chipotle peppers in adobo sauce, peppers diced

⅓ cup (80 ml) honey

⅛ cup (28 g) brown sugar

2 tbsp (30 ml) apple cider vinegar

1 tbsp (15 ml) Worcestershire sauce

1 tsp kosher salt

1 tsp ground black pepper

1 tsp paprika

BRISKET QUESADILLAS

2 cups (480 g) chopped leftover beef brisket (page 27)

8 oz (224 g) goat cheese, softened

1 cup (113 g) shredded sharp Cheddar cheese

8 (10″ [25-cm]) flour tortillas

½ cup (58 g) thinly sliced red onion

1 tbsp (15 ml) olive oil

Honey–Chipotle Brisket and Goat Cheese Quesadillas

I don't often have leftover brisket, but when I do, I like to make something fun with the leftovers. Nothing beats a good quesadilla, especially when it's paired with a delicious homemade BBQ sauce and a creamy goat cheese mixture. You will wish you had made more of these after your last bite is gone. Serve them with your favorite quesadilla toppings, such as cilantro, scallions, avocado and sour cream.

To make the honey-chipotle sauce, heat the olive oil in a medium saucepan over medium heat. Add the onion and let it cook for 2 to 3 minutes. Next, add the garlic and let the mixture cook 1 to 2 minutes, until the garlic is fragrant. Add the remaining ingredients for the honey-chipotle sauce, mix everything together well and reduce the heat to medium-low. Let the sauce cook for 10 to 15 minutes, stirring it often, until it thickens. Use an immersion blender or a countertop blender to blend the sauce to a silky consistency. Store extra sauce in the fridge for 2 weeks.

Set up your Big Green Egg for direct grilling (as described on page 18) using the EGGspander base and the Big Green Egg Half Moon Cast Iron Plancha Griddle, flat side up. Preheat the Big Green Egg to 350°F (177°C). While the Big Green Egg and plancha are preheating, let's assemble the quesadillas.

First, mix the leftover brisket with ½ cup (120 ml) of the honey-chipotle sauce in a medium bowl, and then set the sauced brisket to the side. Next, mix the goat cheese with the Cheddar cheese in a medium bowl and set that bowl to the side. Lay your tortillas on a flat surface. To fill the quesadillas, place one-eighth of the cheese mixture on the bottom half of each tortilla, followed by one-eighth of the brisket on top of the cheese mixture. Top the brisket layer with some of the sliced red onion, and then fold the tortilla in half, pressing down slightly to hold the quesadilla's shape.

Once the Big Green Egg and plancha have preheated, add the olive oil to the plancha and spread it evenly with a metal spatula to coat the plancha with oil. Lay your quesadillas on the plancha. Depending on the size of your Big Green Egg and associated plancha, you may have to cook the quesadillas in batches. Cook the quesadillas for 2 to 3 minutes, until they are nicely browned and crispy. Flip them and cook for 2 to 3 minutes on the other side. When the quesadillas are golden brown on each side, remove them from the plancha and serve.

FEEDS: 4–6 people

APPROXIMATE COOK TIME:
6+ hours to marinate, 10
minutes to cook

BIG GREEN EGG SETUP:
Direct

TOOLS AND ACCESSORIES:
Metal or wooden skewers

PEANUT SAUCE

3 tbsp (48 g) creamy peanut
butter

1 tbsp (15 ml) soy sauce

1 tbsp (15 ml) fresh lime juice

2 tsp (10 g) brown sugar

2 tsp (10 ml) chili-garlic sauce

1 tsp grated fresh ginger

2 tbsp (30 ml) water

Spicy Thai Chicken Skewers

Thai food was the very first Asian cuisine I tried when I was growing up. I'll never forget the first time I had chicken satay with peanut sauce. The tangy grilled meat with that sweet and savory peanut sauce hooked me right away. This is my attempt at re-creating the dish that is seared into my memory. I hope you enjoy it as much as I do!

In a small bowl, mix together the peanut butter, soy sauce, lime juice, brown sugar, chili-garlic sauce, ginger and water until the sauce is smooth. Cover the bowl and place it in the refrigerator until you serve the chicken skewers (the longer it sits in the fridge, the better it tastes).

Trim the chicken thighs of extra fat and sinew, then cut them into 1-inch (2.5-cm) pieces. To make the marinade, put the coconut milk, soy sauce, curry powder, turmeric, lemongrass, shallot, jalapeño, garlic, ginger, brown sugar, fish sauce, vegetable oil, salt and pepper in a food processor and process the ingredients until they are smooth. Place the chicken and marinade in a large ziplock bag and let the chicken marinate for 6 hours (or overnight) in the fridge.

Note: If you are using wooden skewers, soak them for at least 1 hour before using them for the chicken.

Set up your Big Green Egg for direct grilling (as described on page 18). Preheat the Big Green Egg to 400°F (204°C). While the Big Green Egg preheats, make the chicken skewers.

CHICKEN

2 lb (908 g) boneless, skinless chicken thighs

¼ cup (60 ml) full-fat canned coconut milk

2 tbsp (30 ml) soy sauce

2½ tsp (5 g) yellow curry powder

1½ tsp (3 g) ground turmeric

2 stalks lemongrass, white parts only

1 shallot, finely chopped

1 jalapeño, deseeded and finely chopped

3 cloves garlic, minced

1 tbsp (15 g) grated fresh ginger

1 tbsp (14 g) brown sugar

1 tbsp (15 ml) fish sauce

1 tbsp (15 ml) vegetable oil

1 tsp kosher salt

½ tsp ground black pepper (ideally 16 mesh)

Coarsely chopped fresh cilantro

Take the chicken out of the marinade and carefully thread each piece of meat onto a skewer. Do not overcrowd the skewers, as you want the chicken pieces spread out enough that they cook evenly. Once all the skewers are assembled and the Big Green Egg has preheated, place the skewers on the grill grate. Cook the chicken for 4 minutes then flip the skewers and cook the chicken for 4 minutes on the other side. Once the internal temperature of the chicken reaches 165°F (74°C) and the exterior is golden brown and charred, it's time to take the skewers off the Big Green Egg.

Serve the chicken skewers with the peanut sauce and cilantro.

FEEDS: 6 people

APPROXIMATE COOK TIME:
1 hour

BIG GREEN EGG SETUP:
Indirect

TOOLS AND ACCESSORIES:
convEGGtor, medium
baking sheet

SLIDERS

8–10 thin slices bacon

1 lb (454 g) pork tenderloin,
trimmed

½ tsp kosher salt, plus more
as needed

½ tsp ground black pepper,
plus more as needed

12 (¼" [6-mm]-thick) tomato
slices

1 tbsp (15 ml) olive oil

12 King's Hawaiian® sweet
rolls

12 slices Swiss cheese

MORNAY SAUCE

3 tbsp (42 g) butter

3 tbsp (24 g) all-purpose flour

1½ cups (360 ml) milk

½ cup (40 g) shredded
Pecorino Romano cheese

½ tsp Worcestershire sauce

Kosher salt, to taste

Ground black pepper, to
taste

"Hot Brown–Style" Pork Tenderloin Sliders

My wife, a.k.a. Mrs. Buddha, grew up in Louisville, Kentucky. When I first visited her family there, I had my first Hot Brown sandwich at the iconic Brown Hotel. From that moment, I was hooked on the Hot Brown sandwich and the city of Louisville. This is a fun take on the Hot Brown in slider form, replacing the turkey with bacon-wrapped pork tenderloin. It's a fantastic appetizer but could easily be your next meal.

Set up the Big Green Egg for indirect grilling (as described on page 20) using the convEGGtor. Preheat the Big Green Egg to 350°F (177°C). While the Big Green Egg is coming up to temperature, prep your bacon-wrapped pork tenderloin.

Take the bacon out of the packaging and lay the bacon flat on a cutting board, overlapping the slices vertically. There should be enough bacon to wrap the pork tenderloin completely. Tuck the tail of the pork tenderloin in on itself, making an even hunk of meat to wrap in the bacon. Season the pork tenderloin with the salt and pepper, then place it on top of the overlapping bacon near the end of bacon strips closest to you. Roll up the pork tenderloin in the overlapping bacon, sealing the ends of the bacon on one side.

Once the Big Green Egg has preheated and the temperature is stable, place the bacon-wrapped pork tenderloin inside with the seam side on the grill grate. Close the Big Green Egg's lid and cook the pork for 25 to 30 minutes, until the internal temperature reaches 135°F (57°C) and the bacon fat has rendered. While the pork is cooking, make your sauces.

To make the Mornay sauce, melt the butter in a medium saucepan over medium heat. When the butter is melted, whisk in the flour, ensuring the mixture is smooth. Continue cooking the mixture for 2 to 3 minutes, stirring it constantly, being careful not to brown the mixture. Now whisk in the milk a little at a time. Increase the heat to medium-high and bring the mixture to a gentle boil and cook it for 2 to 3 minutes, continuing to whisk the mixture constantly, until it has thickened. Now reduce the heat to low, add the Pecorino Romano cheese and let the sauce cook until the cheese has melted. Remove the saucepan from the heat and add the Worcestershire sauce, salt and pepper. Set the Mornay sauce aside and keep it warm.

(continued)

"Hot Brown–Style" Pork Tenderloin Sliders (continued)

BUTTER SAUCE

½ cup (112 g) butter, melted

1 tsp Worcestershire sauce

2 cloves garlic, minced

1 tsp minced fresh parsley

Kosher, salt to taste

Ground black pepper, to taste

To make the butter sauce, mix together all of the ingredients for the butter sauce in a small bowl. Set the butter sauce aside.

When the pork is ready, remove it from the Big Green Egg, place it on a cutting board and let it rest for 10 minutes. In a medium bowl, toss the tomato slices with the olive oil and then season with salt and pepper. Lay the tomato slices in a single layer on a medium baking sheet. Place the baking sheet in the Big Green Egg and cook the tomatoes for about 5 to 7 minutes, while you prep the sliders.

Place the Hawaiian rolls on a baking sheet and use a large serrated knife to cut the rolls in half lengthwise, removing the tops. Do not separate the rolls from each other. Slice 12 medallions from the bacon-wrapped pork tenderloin that are each about ½ inch (1.3 cm) thick. Place a bacon-wrapped medallion on the bottom half of each of the Hawaiian rolls. Now place the slices of Swiss cheese and cooked tomatoes evenly across the pork-topped Hawaiian rolls. Spoon the Mornay sauce all over the top of the tomato layer.

Place the tops of the Hawaiian rolls on the sliders and spread the butter sauce evenly across the tops of the rolls. Cover the baking sheet with aluminum foil and transfer it to the Big Green Egg. Cook the sliders for 15 minutes, until the cheese has melted. Remove the foil and cook the sliders for 5 minutes, until they are browned. Remove the sliders from the Big Green Egg and serve them to your hungry guests!

MEATBALLS

1 lb (454 g) ground chicken

¼ cup (14 g) panko
breadcrumbs

1 egg white

1 tsp kosher salt

½ tsp ground black pepper

1 (7-oz [196-g]) container
bocconcini mozzarella balls

2 tbsp (6 g) finely chopped
fresh parsley

BUFFALO SAUCE

1 stick unsalted butter

1 cup (240 ml) hot sauce

2 tsp (10 ml) Worcestershire
sauce

1 tsp garlic powder

¼ tsp cayenne

Kosher salt, to taste

Stuffed Buffalo Chicken Meatballs

If you like meatballs and buffalo chicken wings, then you will love this recipe. The best of both worlds come together to make this delicious appetizer that is so much fun to make and eat—you will be sad when the meatballs are all gone.

Set up your Big Green Egg for indirect grilling (as described on page 20) using the convEGGtor. Preheat the Big Green Egg to 350°F (177°C). Place a 12-inch (30-cm) cast-iron skillet in the Big Green Egg to preheat.

While the Big Green Egg is coming up to temperature, mix together the ground chicken, panko breadcrumbs, egg white, salt and pepper in a medium bowl. Now form eight golf ball–sized balls with the meat mixture and place them on a baking sheet. Flatten a meatball until it is about ½ inch (1.3 cm) thick, and then place one bocconcini mozzarella ball in the middle of the meat. Fold the meat up and around the mozzarella until you have a chicken meatball that is now stuffed with the cheese. Do this for each of the chicken meatballs you have formed.

Spray a wire baking rack with cooking spray. Place the meatballs on the rack in a single layer, making sure they are evenly spaced. Place the wire baking rack in the preheated Big Green Egg and let the meatballs cook for 15 minutes. Flip the meatballs and cook them for another 15 minutes, until they are nicely browned all over. Remove the wire baking rack from the Big Green Egg and set the meatballs to the side while you make the sauce.

Melt the butter in the preheated cast-iron skillet. Add the hot sauce, Worcestershire sauce, garlic powder, cayenne and salt. Mix the ingredients until they are well combined and let the sauce cook for 10 minutes, until it is warm.

Add the meatballs to the cast-iron skillet, close the lid of the Big Green Egg and allow the meatballs to warm in the sauce for 8 to 10 minutes. Remove the skillet from the Big Green Egg and garnish the meatballs with the parsley.

FEEDS: 4–6 people

APPROXIMATE COOK TIME:
1 hour

BIG GREEN EGG SETUP:
Indirect

TOOLS AND ACCESSORIES:
convEGGtor

HANOI SAUCE

2 cups (32 g) coarsely
chopped fresh cilantro

4 cloves garlic, minced

1 shallot, minced

2 tbsp (30 ml) fish sauce

Juice of 1 lime

1 jalapeño, finely chopped

2 tbsp (30 g) sugar

6 tbsp (84 g) unsalted butter,
melted

CHICKEN

2 lb (908 g) chicken wings

1 tbsp (15 ml) olive oil

Kosher salt

Ground black pepper (ideally
16 mesh)

Coarsely chopped fresh
cilantro

Grilled Hanoi–Style Chicken Wings

This is such an easy and scrumptious wing recipe to make. The sauce is perfectly balanced, and the presentation is gorgeous. Have plenty of napkins on hand for this pile of deliciousness.

Set up your Big Green Egg for indirect grilling (as described on page 20) using the convEGGtor. Preheat the Big Green Egg to 375°F (191°C). While the Big Green Egg is preheating, make your sauce and prepare your chicken wings.

To make the Hanoi sauce, put the cilantro, garlic, shallot, fish sauce, lime juice, jalapeño and sugar in a food processor and process the ingredients until the sauce is smooth. Set the sauce aside until the wings are finished.

Take the wings out of the packaging, dry them with a paper towel and separate the drums from the flats, discarding the wing tips. In a large bowl, toss the wings with the olive oil and season them liberally with salt and pepper.

Once the Big Green Egg has preheated and the temperature is stable, place the wings on the grill grate and cook them for 25 minutes. Flip the wings and cook them for 25 minutes on the other side.

Add the butter to the Hanoi sauce. Remove the wings from the Big Green Egg, place them in a clean large bowl and toss them with the sauce. Put the sauced wings back on the Big Green Egg and cook them for 5 to 10 minutes to set the sauce.

When the wings are nicely browned and crispy, remove them from the Big Green Egg and garnish them with the cilantro.

FEEDS: 3–6 people

APPROXIMATE COOK TIME: 4+ hours to marinate, 6 minutes to cook

BIG GREEN EGG SETUP: Direct

TOOLS AND ACCESSORIES: None

CHIMICHURRI

1 shallot, finely chopped

1 Fresno chile, finely chopped

5 cloves garlic, finely chopped

½ cup (120 ml) red wine vinegar

1 tsp kosher salt

½ cup (8 g) minced fresh cilantro

¼ cup (12 g) minced fresh parsley

2 tsp (2 g) dried oregano

¾ cup (180 ml) extra-virgin olive oil

LAMB LOLLIPOPS

6 (¾" [19-mm]-thick) lamb chops, Frenched

Kosher salt

Ground black pepper (ideally 16 mesh)

Avocado oil or neutral cooking oil, for grill grate

Lamb Lollipops with Cilantro Chimichurri

Lamb lollipops are such a great way to start a gathering. If you are grilling something else for the main course, this is the perfect appetizer to use. A quick, easy sear on each side and—boom!—the guests are served. Paired with a bright chimichurri sauce, these lamb lollipops are bursting with flavor in every bite.

To make the chimichurri, combine the shallot, chile, garlic, red wine vinegar and salt in a small bowl. Let this mixture sit for 10 minutes. Then stir in the cilantro, parsley and oregano. Next, use a fork to whisk in the olive oil slowly, ensuring the mixture does not separate. Transfer ½ cup (120 ml) of the chimichurri to a small bowl and reserve it for serving.

Place the lamb lollipops in a large ziplock bag and pour in the remaining chimichurri. Use your hands to move the lamb around in the marinade, making sure that the lamb is coated evenly. Place the bag in the refrigerator and let the lamb marinate for 4 hours or overnight (the longer, the better).

Set up your Big Green Egg for direct grilling (as described on page 18). Preheat the grill to 450°F (232°C). While the Big Green Egg is preheating, prep your lamb lollipops.

Take the lamb lollipops out of the marinade, pat them dry, season them with the salt and pepper and wrap the exposed bones with a piece of aluminum foil. When the Big Green Egg has preheated and the temperature it stable, oil the grill grate with a paper towel that has been dipped in the avocado oil to ensure that the chops don't stick, then place the lamb on the grill grate. Make sure to wear heat-resistant gloves when you do this. Cook the lamb 2 to 3 minutes, until the meat is nicely browned and slightly charred. Flip the lamb lollipops and cook them for 2 to 3 minutes on the other side.

Remove the lamb from the Big Green Egg, remove the foil from the bones and serve the lamb lollipops with the reserved chimichurri sauce for dipping.

FEEDS: 4 people

APPROXIMATE COOK TIME:
40 minutes

BIG GREEN EGG SETUP:
Indirect

TOOLS AND ACCESSORIES:
convEGGtor, wire baking
rack

GARLIC AIOLI

¾ cup (180 ml) mayonnaise

3 cloves garlic, minced

2 tbsp (30 ml) fresh lemon juice

1 tsp kosher salt

½ tsp ground black pepper

1 tbsp (3 g) finely chopped fresh parsley

POTATOES

2 russet potatoes

1 tbsp (12 g) your favorite BBQ rub (I used Dizzy Pig Crossroads)

16 thin slices bacon

Bacon–Wrapped Taters with Garlic Aioli

This hearty appetizer is easy and sure to please. Fluffy, tender potatoes wrapped in crispy bacon marry well with the zippy garlic aioli. This appetizer is the perfect game day treat, especially on a cool fall day.

To make the garlic aioli, mix together the mayonnaise, garlic, lemon juice, salt, pepper and parsley in a small bowl. Refrigerate the aioli until you are ready to serve.

Set up your Big Green Egg for indirect grilling (as described on page 20) using the convEGGtor. Preheat the Big Green Egg to 375°F (191°C). While your Big Green Egg is preheating, prep your bacon-wrapped potatoes.

Wash the potatoes well and cut each of them lengthwise into eight thick wedges. Season the potato wedges liberally with your favorite BBQ rub. Wrap each potato wedge with a slice of bacon, securing the bacon with a toothpick as needed. Place the bacon-wrapped potato wedges on a wire baking rack and spray them lightly with cooking spray.

When your Big Green Egg has preheated, place the potato wedges, still on the wire baking rack, the grill grate. Cook the potatoes for 40 minutes, turning them halfway through the cooking time. When the bacon is nicely browned and crispy, remove the rack with the potatoes, allow them to cool slightly and serve them with the garlic aioli for dipping.

FEEDS: 4–6 people

APPROXIMATE COOK TIME:
45 minutes

BIG GREEN EGG SETUP:
Direct

TOOLS AND ACCESSORIES:
Big Green Egg Half Moon
Perforated Cooking Grid

5 plum tomatoes, halved

½ white onion, cut into
wedges

2 jalapeños, stems removed

2 cloves garlic, minced

1 tbsp (15 ml) olive oil

Juice of 1 lime

½ bunch fresh cilantro,
coarsely chopped

1 tsp ground cumin

1 tsp kosher salt, plus more
as needed

½ tsp ground black pepper

Charred Tomato Salsa

Nothing beats the taste of homemade salsa. Making salsa using your Big Green Egg is even better, as the charred vegetables create an amazing depth of flavor and texture. Once you make this recipe, you will never buy salsa from the store again.

Set up your Big Green Egg for direct grilling (as described on page 18) and preheat it to 400°F (204°C). While the Big Green Egg preheats, place the Big Green Egg Half Moon Perforated Cooking Grid on the grill grate to preheat as well. While the Big Green Egg and the grid are preheating, prepare your vegetables.

In a medium bowl, combine the tomatoes, onion, jalapeños and garlic. Toss the vegetables in the olive oil to coat them well. When the Big Green Egg has preheated, place the vegetables on the grid. Cook the vegetables for 10 to 15 minutes, or until they are nicely charred, turning them frequently. When you see the char and like the color of your roasted vegetables, pull them off the Big Green Egg and let them cool for 20 to 30 minutes.

Once the vegetables have cooled, place them in a food processor along with the lime juice, cilantro, cumin, salt and pepper. Pulse until you have a chunky consistency (pulse more if you like your salsa thinner). Taste the salsa and add more salt as needed.

Serve the salsa with tortilla chips for a delicious summer appetizer.

FEEDS: 4–8 people

APPROXIMATE COOK TIME: 2 hours

BIG GREEN EGG SETUP: Indirect

SUGGESTED WOOD TYPE: Apple or pecan chunks

TOOLS AND ACCESSORIES: convEGGtor, 13″ (33-cm) rectangular drip pan, 12″ (30-cm) cast-iron skillet

CREAM CHEESE

2 (8-oz [224-g]) blocks cream cheese

BBQ rub of your choice (I used Dizzy Pig Dizzy Dust)

BOURBON–BACON JAM

12 oz (336 g) bacon, diced

1 yellow onion, diced

3 cloves garlic, minced

⅔ cup (160 ml) apple cider vinegar

6 tbsp (84 g) brown sugar

¼ cup (60 ml) bourbon

⅓ cup (80 ml) water

1 Fresno chile

Ground black pepper, to taste

Smoked Cream Cheese with Bourbon–Bacon Jam

This appetizer was all the rage last year on social media, and in my book, this trend should stick around because it is crazy delicious. Smoking cream cheese is easier than it sounds and well worth the wait. When the smoked cream cheese is paired with this well-balanced bourbon-bacon jam, you will leave your guests wanting more when it is gone!

Set up your Big Green Egg for indirect grilling (as described on page 20) using the convEGGtor. Mix in two chunks of apple or pecan wood with the lump charcoal for smoke flavor. Preheat the Big Green Egg to 225°F (107°C). While the Big Green Egg is preheating, prep the cream cheese.

Line a 13-inch (33-cm) rectangular drip pan with aluminum foil, and then place the blocks of cream cheese in the pan, making sure they are evenly spaced. Cut a ¼-inch (6-mm)-deep crosshatch pattern on the tops of the blocks of cream cheese. Top the blocks of cream cheese with your favorite BBQ rub and place them in your preheated Big Green Egg. Let the cream cheese smoke for 2 hours, until it is nicely browned. While the cream cheese is smoking, make the bourbon-bacon jam.

On your stove, heat a 12-inch (30-cm) cast-iron skillet over medium heat. Add the bacon and sauté it for about 10 minutes, until it is crispy. Remove the bacon from the skillet and drain all but 1 tablespoon (15 ml) of the bacon grease. Add the onion and garlic and cook them for about 3 minutes, until they are tender and fragrant. Next, add the apple cider vinegar, brown sugar, bourbon, water, chile and pepper. Mix the ingredients together well and bring the mixture to a gentle boil. Reduce the heat to medium-low to maintain a simmer and cook the mixture for about 15 minutes, stirring it occasionally, until the liquid is mostly cooked off. When the mixture is thick and syrupy, it is ready. Pull the bourbon-bacon jam off the heat and set it aside until the cream cheese is ready.

After 2 hours, remove the blocks of smoked cream cheese from the Big Green Egg, place them on a serving tray, top them with the bourbon-bacon jam, open a bag of your favorite crackers and enjoy!

APPROXIMATE COOK TIME:
2 hours

BIG GREEN EGG SETUP:
Indirect

SUGGESTED WOOD TYPE:
Apple or pecan chips

TOOLS AND ACCESSORIES:
convEGGtor

12 eggs

¾ cup (180 ml) mayonnaise

1 tsp dry mustard

1 tsp distilled white vinegar

½ tsp cayenne

1 tsp kosher salt

½ tsp ground black pepper

½ tsp smoked paprika

6 strips bacon, cooked and
chopped into large pieces

Deviled Eggs with Bacon

This is my go-to deviled egg recipe for any springtime party or get-together. The deviled eggs I make are pretty classic, with one exception . . . I smoke the eggs first! You read that correctly—I smoke the eggs, then I make the deviled eggs. This added dimension of smoke flavor makes people take a second look after their first bite and will have them reaching for more.

Set up the Big Green Egg for indirect grilling (as described on page 20) using the convEGGtor. Load the Big Green Egg with natural lump charcoal and mix in two handfuls of apple or pecan wood chips with the lump charcoal. Now light the lump charcoal and preheat the Big Green Egg to 225°F (107°C).

When the Big Green Egg has preheated and the smoke is light gray in color, place the whole eggs directly on the grill grate. Smoke the whole eggs undisturbed for 2 hours. At the 2-hour mark, remove the eggs from the Big Green Egg and place them in an ice bath to cool down. Once the eggs are chilled, remove them from the ice bath and peel them.

Slice the eggs in half lengthwise and carefully transfer the smoked yolks to a medium bowl. Add the mayonnaise, mustard, vinegar, cayenne, salt, pepper and paprika. Mix the ingredients together well but not too smoothly. Now use a spoon to gently fill each egg half with approximately 1 tablespoon (15 g) of the egg yolk mixture. Top each deviled egg with a piece of cooked bacon and enjoy!

FEEDS: 6 people

APPROXIMATE COOK TIME:
1 hour

BIG GREEN EGG SETUP:
Indirect

TOOLS AND ACCESSORIES:
convEGGtor

HOISIN GLAZE

1 cup (240 ml) hoisin sauce

¼ cup (60 ml) soy sauce

2 tbsp (30 ml) honey

1 tbsp (15 ml) rice wine vinegar

2 tbsp (30 ml) toasted sesame oil

2 tbsp (30 g) minced fresh ginger

4 cloves garlic, minced

1 tbsp (15 ml) chili-garlic sauce

1 tsp Chinese five-spice powder

CHICKEN DRUMSTICKS

1 tsp kosher salt

1 tsp ground black pepper (ideally 16 mesh)

1 tsp garlic powder

3 lb (1.4 kg) chicken drumsticks

Thinly sliced scallion tops

Toasted sesame seeds

Hoisin–Glazed Chicken Drumsticks

Chicken drumsticks are becoming more popular thanks to the high demand and price of chicken wings these days. When done right, chicken drumsticks are every bit as satisfying as their chicken wing counterparts. Be sure to try these drumsticks—the Chinese-inspired glaze will leave you wanting more.

Set up the Big Green Egg for indirect grilling (as described on page 20) using the convEGGtor. Preheat the Big Green Egg to 350°F (177°C). While the Big Green Egg is coming up to temperature, prep the glaze and chicken drumsticks.

In a small saucepan over medium heat, combine all of the ingredients for the hoisin glaze and bring the mixture to a slight boil. Reduce the heat to medium-low and let the mixture simmer for 15 to 20 minutes. Remove the glaze from the heat and set it aside.

In a large bowl, combine the salt, pepper and garlic powder. Add the chicken drumsticks and mix the ingredients well to coat the drumsticks. When the Big Green Egg has preheated and the temperature is stable, place the seasoned drumsticks in the Big Green Egg to cook. Cook the drumsticks for 15 minutes, then flip them and cook them for another 15 minutes. When the internal temperature of the drumsticks reaches 165°F (74°C), pull them from the Big Green Egg and glaze them liberally with the hoisin glaze. Put them back on the Big Green Egg and cook them for 5 to 10 minutes, until the sauce sets.

Pull the drumsticks from the Big Green Egg, and then garnish them with the scallions and sesame seeds.

CHAPTER 7

Keep It Simple

SIDES, VEGGIES AND CARBS

The Big Green Egg does much more than smoke or grill meat! For your next grilled dinner, cook up some vegetables and sides—and get ready to be blown away by how easy and flavorful they are. The added layers of flavor you get from cooking in a live-fire environment is second to none. The recipes in this chapter will complete any BBQ dinner you have planned for friends and family. They are so good, they could even stand on their own as main dishes when you're in the mood for a light and fresh meal.

FEEDS: 4 people

APPROXIMATE COOK TIME:
15 minutes

BIG GREEN EGG SETUP:
Direct grilling

TOOLS AND ACCESSORIES:
Metal or wooden skewers,
Big Green Egg Half Moon
Perforated Cooking Grid

ASIAN-STYLE SAUCE

¼ cup (60 ml) soy sauce

2 tbsp (30 ml) fish sauce

1 tbsp (15 ml) sriracha

1 tbsp (3 g) finely chopped
scallions

1 tsp red pepper flakes

1 tsp kosher salt

1 tsp ground black pepper

VEGGIES

2 zucchini, cut into 1" (2.5-cm)
pieces

2 white onions, cut into
1" (2.5-cm) pieces

1 pint (275 g) cherry tomatoes

1 lb (454 g) button
mushrooms

1 red bell pepper, cut into
1" (2.5-cm) pieces

1 green bell pepper, cut into
1" (2.5-cm) pieces

1 yellow bell pepper, cut into
1" (2.5-cm) pieces

1½ tbsp (23 ml) avocado oil

Ground black pepper, to taste

Kosher salt, to taste

Asian–Style Veggie Kebabs

This recipe is the second one I created with my daughter, Jessica (@agranolacoconut on Instagram). It's the perfect side dish or vegetarian main for your next backyard BBQ, especially one featuring other Asian-inspired dishes. The combination of flavors between the charred vegetable kebabs and the Asian-style sauce is so good you will wish you had made twice as much.

If you are using wooden skewers, soak them for at least 1 hour before using them for the veggies.

Set up the Big Green Egg for direct grilling (as described on page 18) and preheat it to 400°F (204°C). Place the Big Green Egg Half Moon Perforated Cooking Grid on the grill while it is preheating. While the Big Green Egg is coming up to temperature, make the Asian-style sauce.

In a small bowl, mix together all of the ingredients for the Asian-style sauce. Set the sauce aside while you assemble the skewers and cook the vegetables.

On the skewers, alternate pieces of the zucchini, onion, tomatoes, mushrooms, red bell pepper, green bell pepper and yellow bell pepper. Fill the skewers until all the vegetables are used.

Once the Big Green Egg has preheated, place the skewers on the grid. Cook the vegetables for 2 to 3 minutes, and then flip the skewers and cook the vegetables for 2 to 3 minutes on the other side. When the vegetables are nicely charred and tender, remove the skewers from the Big Green Egg, add a bit of pepper and some salt and top the vegetables with the Asian-style sauce.

FEEDS: 4 people

APPROXIMATE COOK TIME:
1 hour

BIG GREEN EGG SETUP:
Indirect

TOOLS AND ACCESSORIES:
convEGGtor, large baking
sheet

SALSA VERDE

1 shallot, diced

3 tbsp (45 ml) red wine
vinegar

¼ cup (12 g) minced fresh
parsley

¼ cup (60 ml) olive oil

1 clove garlic, minced

1 tsp red pepper flakes

Kosher salt, to taste

POTATOES

2 lb (908 g) red potatoes

1 tbsp (18 g) plus 1 tsp kosher
salt, divided

2 tbsp (30 ml) olive oil

Smashed Red Potatoes with Salsa Verde

This is a fun side dish to make, as you get to smash all the potatoes before putting them in the Big Green Egg. Crispy and delicious, these potatoes are the perfect side dish for any meal. And when your dinner guests dip the potatoes in the salsa verde, their taste buds will be overwhelmed.

Set up the Big Green Egg for indirect grilling (as described on page 20) using the convEGGtor. Preheat the Big Green Egg to 425°F (218°C). While the Big Green Egg is coming up to temperature, make your salsa verde.

In a small bowl, mix together all of the ingredients for the salsa verde until they are well combined. Cover the bowl and leave it in the refrigerator until the potatoes are ready.

To prepare the potatoes, place the potatoes in a large pot and fill it with water until the water covers the potatoes by 1 inch (2.5 cm). Add 1 tablespoon (18 g) of the salt and bring the pot of water to a boil over medium-high heat. Continue to boil the potatoes for 15 to 20 minutes, until they are tender and easily pierced with a fork. Drain the potatoes in a colander and let them cool for 5 minutes before proceeding.

Place the potatoes on a large baking sheet, making sure the potatoes are evenly spaced. Using the bottom of a drinking glass, press down firmly on the potatoes, smashing them to a thickness of ½ inch (1.3 cm). Drizzle the potatoes with the olive oil and sprinkle them with the remaining 1 teaspoon of salt.

Once the Big Green Egg has preheated, place the baking sheet on the grill grate. Cook the potatoes for 25 to 30 minutes, until the potatoes are nicely browned and crispy. Remove the potatoes from the Big Green Egg, let them cool for 5 minutes and serve them with the salsa verde.

FEEDS: 4 people

APPROXIMATE COOK TIME:
15 minutes

BIG GREEN EGG SETUP:
Two-zone grilling

TOOLS AND ACCESSORIES:
None

HERB AND CUCUMBER YOGURT DRIZZLE

¼ cup (36 g) golden raisins

1½ cups (360 ml) plain unsweetened yogurt

1 English cucumber, peeled and shredded

2 tbsp (12 g) minced fresh mint

2 tbsp (6 g) minced fresh parsley

2 cloves garlic, minced

¼ cup (34 g) roasted and lightly salted sunflower seeds

2 tbsp (30 ml) olive oil

½ tsp kosher salt

CARROTS

1 lb (454 g) carrots

1 tbsp (15 ml) olive oil

Grilled Carrots with Herb and Cucumber Yogurt Drizzle

This is an easy and satisfying grilled vegetable dish. The sweetness of the carrots is accentuated by the char from the Big Green Egg. Paired with the herb and cucumber yogurt drizzle, this dish really shines. It's a satisfying side for your next summer grilling session.

Set up the Big Green Egg for two-zone grilling (as described on page 20) and preheat it to 350°F (177°C). While the Big Green is coming up to temperature, start prepping the herb and cucumber yogurt drizzle.

In a medium bowl, combine all of the ingredients for the herb and cucumber yogurt drizzle. Mix the ingredients together well, then let the yogurt drizzle chill in the refrigerator until the carrots are ready.

Clean and trim your carrots, and then place them in a medium bowl. If any of the carrots are very thick, split them in half lengthwise. Toss the carrots with the olive oil and set them aside.

When the Big Green Egg has preheated, place the carrots on the direct side of the grill grate and cook them for 12 to 15 minutes, turning them frequently, until a nice, even char develops. If the grill is too hot and the carrots are cooking too fast, move them to the indirect side of the grill to finish cooking.

When the carrots have developed a nice charred color and are easily pierced with a fork, remove them from the Big Green Egg. Allow them to cool for 5 minutes then drizzle them with the herb and cucumber yogurt.

FEEDS: 4 people

APPROXIMATE COOK TIME:
25 minutes

BIG GREEN EGG SETUP:
Raised direct grilling

TOOLS AND ACCESSORIES:
12″ (30-cm) cast-iron
skillet

4 slices bacon

1 lb (454 g) fresh Brussels
sprouts

1 tbsp (14 g) butter

4 cloves garlic, minced

½ tsp kosher salt

½ tsp ground black pepper

1 tbsp (15 ml) honey

⅓ cup (37 g) crumbled
goat cheese

Brussels Sprouts with Honey, Bacon and Warm Goat Cheese

This delicious recipe is the perfect side dish for your next dinner. The tender Brussels sprouts are nicely charred and pair beautifully with the honey, bacon and goat cheese. Even the harshest Brussels sprouts critic will enjoy this dish.

Set up the Big Green Egg for raised direct grilling (as described on page 18), and preheat it to 400°F (204°C). Place a 12-inch (30-cm) cast-iron skillet on the grill grate to preheat with the Big Green Egg. While the Big Green Egg is coming up to temperature, cook the bacon.

When the cast-iron skillet is hot, place the bacon in the skillet and cook it for 8 to 12 minutes, turning the bacon over halfway through the cooking time. As the bacon cooks, cut the stems off the Brussels sprouts, rinse them and split them in half lengthwise. Pat them dry and set them aside.

When the bacon is done, transfer the bacon to a plate lined with paper towels to drain and cool. Once the bacon is cool, chop it into small pieces.

Remove all the bacon fat from the cast-iron skillet except for 1 tablespoon (15 ml) to cook with. Add the butter to the cast-iron skillet. When the butter has melted, add the garlic, salt and pepper. Next, place the Brussels sprouts in the skillet cut side down, close the dome of the Big Green Egg and cook the Brussels sprouts undisturbed for 5 minutes. Now open the dome and stir the Brussels sprouts to mix them well with the butter and oil in the skillet. Close the dome and cook the Brussels sprouts for another 5 minutes, until they are nicely charred and tender.

Remove the cast-iron skillet from the Big Green Egg. Stir in the chopped bacon, drizzle the honey over the top of the Brussels sprouts and sprinkle the goat cheese all over them.

FEEDS: 4 people

APPROXIMATE COOK TIME:
15 minutes

BIG GREEN EGG SETUP:
Direct grilling

TOOLS AND ACCESSORIES:
None

ASIAN CHIMICHURRI

2 tbsp (6 g) minced fresh parsley

2 tbsp (2 g) minced fresh cilantro

2 tbsp (6 g) minced scallions

1 tsp grated fresh ginger

1 clove garlic, minced

1 tsp red pepper flakes

1 tbsp (15 ml) soy sauce

¼ cup (60 ml) avocado oil

3 tbsp (45 ml) seasoned rice wine vinegar

CAULIFLOWER STEAKS

2 heads cauliflower

¼ cup (60 ml) olive oil

1 tsp kosher salt

¼ tsp ground black pepper

½ tsp smoked paprika

Cauliflower Steaks with Asian Chimichurri

This vegetable dish is so good it can stand on its own as an entrée. However, as this is a book mostly about BBQ, I have kept this recipe in the veggies and sides section. The charred cauliflower pairs nicely with the bright flavors in this Asian-inspired chimichurri. You will find other uses for this topping, as it also complements shrimp, chicken and seafood.

Set up the Big Green Egg for direct grilling (as described on page 18) and preheat it to 400°F (204°C). While the Big Green Egg is coming up to temperature, make your Asian chimichurri.

In a medium bowl, combine all of the ingredients for the Asian chimichurri. Mix the ingredients together well, and then set aside as you cook your cauliflower steaks.

Place one of the cauliflower heads on a cutting board and remove the outer leaves. Cut out the bottom stem and set the cauliflower upright on the cutting board. Cut the head of cauliflower vertically into two thick steaks that are each 1 to 1½ inches (2.5 to 4 cm) thick. Do this with the second head of cauliflower, leaving you with four steaks to grill. Brush each steak with some of the olive oil and season each one with the salt, pepper and smoked paprika.

When the Big Green Egg has preheated and the temperature is stable, carefully place the cauliflower steaks on the grill grate and cook them for 5 to 6 minutes, until you see a nice char forming on the bottom of the steaks. Flip the cauliflower steaks and cook them for 5 to 6 minutes on the other side.

When you see that the cauliflower steaks have a nice char and they are slightly soft to the touch, remove them from the grill. Let the cauliflower steaks cool for 5 minutes then drizzle the Asian chimichurri over them.

APPROXIMATE COOK TIME:
10–15 minutes

BIG GREEN EGG SETUP:
Direct

TOOLS AND ACCESSORIES:
None

2 jalapeños

4 ears corn

1 tbsp (15 ml) olive oil

1 tsp kosher salt

½ tsp ground black pepper

2 tbsp (30 ml) mayonnaise

1 tbsp (15 ml) sour cream

2 oz (56 g) cotija cheese, crumbled, plus more as needed

½ cup (25 g) thinly sliced scallions

½ cup (8 g) coarsely chopped fresh cilantro leaves, plus more as needed

3 cloves garlic, minced

Juice of 1 lime

Chili powder, to taste

Grilled Mexican Corn Salad

If you like elotes, you will love this side dish. This recipe has all the vibrant flavors of Mexican street corn but none of the mess. This will be a side dish you will go to time and time again.

Set up your Big Green Egg for direct grilling (as described on page 18) and preheat it to 400°F (204°C). While your Big Green Egg is preheating, prep your ingredients.

First, deseed the jalapeños and place them in a large bowl. Next, husk and clean the corn and place the ears of corn in the same bowl with the jalapeños. Toss the jalapeños and corn with the olive oil, salt and pepper. When the Big Green Egg is ready, place the corn and jalapeños on the grill grate. Cook the vegetables for 8 to 10 minutes, turning them frequently, until they are browned and slightly charred. Remove the vegetables from the Big Green Egg and allow them to cool.

While the grilled ingredients are cooling, mix together the mayonnaise, sour cream, cotija cheese, scallions, cilantro, garlic and lime juice in a large bowl to make the dressing. When the jalapeños have cooled, dice them and add them to the dressing. Slice the roasted corn kernels from the ears and add them to the dressing as well.

Mix the salad well and serve it, topped with the additional cotija, additional cilantro and chili powder, in a large bowl.

Eggplant Parmesan Boats

This is one of my favorite vegetarian dishes to make on the Big Green Egg. This recipe is packed with flavor and makes for a hearty meal. Your guests will be wanting more when the last piece has been happily devoured.

FEEDS: 4 people

APPROXIMATE COOK TIME:
1½ hours

BIG GREEN EGG SETUP:
Indirect

TOOLS AND ACCESSORIES:
convEGGtor, wire baking rack, 13″ (33-cm) rectangular drip pan

2 eggplants

10 tbsp (150 ml) olive oil, divided

1 tbsp (18 g) kosher salt, plus more as needed

1 tbsp (6 g) ground black pepper, plus more as needed

1 yellow onion, diced

10 cloves garlic, minced

1 (28-oz [784-g]) can San Marzano tomatoes, undrained

4 tsp (4 g) dried oregano

1½ cups (84 g) coarse panko breadcrumbs

2 cups (224 g) shredded mozzarella cheese

½ cup (50 g) grated Parmesan cheese

2 tbsp (2 g) coarsely chopped fresh basil

1 tbsp (6 g) shredded Parmesan cheese

1 tsp red pepper flakes

Set up your Big Green Egg for indirect grilling (as described on page 20) using the convEGGtor. Preheat the Big Green Egg to 400°F (204°C).

Cut the eggplants in half lengthwise and fold each one open like a book. Using a spoon, scoop out all the eggplants' inner flesh, leaving about ½ inch (1.3 cm) of flesh around the skin. Coarsely chop the eggplant flesh and set it aside for the filling later. Place the eggplant boats on a baking sheet and toss them with 6 tablespoons (90 ml) of the olive oil, salt and pepper. When they have been oiled and seasoned, place the boats on a wire baking rack cut side down. Place the wire rack in your preheated Big Green Egg and cook the eggplant boats for 30 to 40 minutes, until they are soft.

While the eggplant boats are cooking, heat 2 tablespoons (30 ml) of the olive oil in a 12-inch (30-cm) skillet over medium heat. Add the onion and cook it for 5 to 6 minutes, stirring it frequently, until it is translucent and slightly browned. Next, add the garlic and cook the mixture for 1 to 2 minutes, stirring it frequently, until the garlic is fragrant. Now add the reserved chopped eggplant and cook the mixture for 3 to 4 minutes. Add the tomatoes and their liquid, crushing the tomatoes with the backside of a spoon or a fork as you fold them into the eggplant mixture. Add the oregano, additional salt and additional pepper to taste. Simmer the filling uncovered for 20 to 30 minutes, until it has thickened. In a medium bowl, combine the panko breadcrumbs with 2 tablespoons (30 ml) of the olive oil. Mix them together well and set the bowl to the side.

Remove the eggplant boats from the Big Green Egg and place them cut side up in a 13-inch (33-cm) rectangular drip pan. Fill the boats with the eggplant-tomato filling and top each boat with the mozzarella cheese. Sprinkle the panko mixture and the grated Parmesan cheese on top of the mozzarella. Place the eggplant boats, still in the drip pan, back in the Big Green Egg and cook them for 20 minutes or so, until the mozzarella is nicely melted and the breadcrumbs are toasted.

Remove the eggplant boats and garnish them with the basil, shredded Parmesan cheese and red pepper flakes.

FEEDS: 4–6 people

APPROXIMATE COOK TIME:
30 minutes

BIG GREEN EGG SETUP:
Direct

TOOLS AND ACCESSORIES:
Big Green Egg Half Moon
Perforated Cooking Grid

3 tbsp (54 g) plus 1 tsp kosher
salt, divided

2 lb (908 g) red potatoes

1 tbsp (15 ml) olive oil, plus
more as needed

1 tsp garlic powder

1 tsp ground black pepper

1 tbsp (3 g) finely chopped
fresh parsley

Herbed Red Potatoes

I love grilled potatoes in the summer. My secret is to parboil them just slightly to enable the time on the grill to be most effective for that tender middle and crispy skin we all love. This quick and easy recipe will deliver perfectly grilled potatoes every time. It pairs nicely with steak grilled on the Big Green Egg. You can parboil and cool the potatoes before grilling your steak, then while the steak is resting, pop the potatoes on the hot grill for the perfect summer dinner.

Fill a large pot with water and 3 tablespoons (54 g) of the salt. Bring the water to a boil over medium-high heat, and then add the potatoes to the pot. Boil the potatoes for 7 minutes, then drain them and transfer them to a large bowl. Let the potatoes cool in the fridge for 20 to 30 minutes. Toss the cooled potatoes with the olive oil, remaining 1 teaspoon of salt, garlic powder and pepper.

Set up your Big Green Egg for direct grilling (as described on page 18) and preheat it to 400°F (204°C). While the Big Green Egg preheats, place the Big Green Egg Half Moon Perforated Cooking Grid on the grill grate to preheat as well.

When the Big Green Egg has preheated, place the potatoes on the preheated grid and cook them for 10 to 15 minutes, until they nicely browned and charred. Pull the potatoes from the Big Green Egg and, in a large serving bowl, toss them with a little additional olive oil and the parsley. Serve and enjoy!

APPROXIMATE COOK TIME:
20 minutes

BIG GREEN EGG SETUP:
Direct

TOOLS AND ACCESSORIES:
Big Green Egg Half Moon
Perforated Cooking Grid

1 red bell pepper, deseeded
and diced into 1″ (2.5-cm)
pieces

1 yellow bell pepper,
deseeded and diced into
1″ (2.5-cm) pieces

1 zucchini, cut in to 1″
(2.5-cm) pieces

1 red onion, quartered

1 ear corn, husked, cleaned
and cut into 2″ (5-cm) rounds

1 tbsp (15 ml) olive oil

1 tsp kosher salt

1 tsp garlic powder

1 tsp ground black pepper

1 tbsp (3 g) finely chopped
fresh parsley

Grilled Summer Vegetables

Sometimes you need to let the ingredients do the talking. When it is summertime and vegetables are at their peak freshness, I know what I am doing for a side dish. This simple yet delicious recipe will be in your regular summer rotation.

Set up your Big Green Egg for direct grilling (as described on page 18) and preheat it to 400°F (204°C). While the Big Green Egg preheats, place the Big Green Egg Half Moon Perforated Cooking Grid on the grill grate to preheat as well.

In a large bowl, mix the vegetables together with the olive oil, salt, garlic powder and pepper. Once the Big Green Egg has preheated, carefully remove the preheated perforated half-moon pan using a heat-resistant glove and spray it with cooking oil spray. Place it back on to the grill grate and pour the vegetables onto the grid. Close the Big Green Egg's dome and cook the vegetables for 2 to 4 minutes.

Open the Big Green Egg and begin to toss the vegetables around, ensuring you are getting a nice sear on all sides. Cook the vegetables for 8 to 10 minutes, until they are browned all over yet still crisp. Remove the vegetables from the Big Green Egg and toss them with the parsley.

FEEDS: 4 people

APPROXIMATE COOK TIME:
1 hour

BIG GREEN EGG SETUP:
Indirect

TOOLS AND ACCESSORIES:
convEGGtor, chopsticks,
12" (30-cm) cast-iron
skillet

4 russet potatoes

1 stick butter, softened

½ cup (120 ml) extra-virgin
olive oil

¼ cup (40 g) finely chopped
shallots

2 tbsp (6 g) minced fresh
parsley, plus more as needed

4 cloves garlic, minced

Herbed–Butter Hasselback Potatoes

This classic side dish is a must-have for any Big Green Egg owner. Crispy on the outside and tender on the inside, Hasselback potatoes are always delicious. Topped with a decadent herbed butter, these potatoes are a perfect side dish for the many tasty grilled recipes featured in this book.

Set up the Big Green Egg for indirect grilling (as described on page 20). Preheat the Big Green Egg to 400°F (204°C). While the Big Green Egg is coming up to temperature, prep your potatoes.

Lay two chopsticks on a flat surface and place the potatoes between them (the chopsticks act as a guide so you do not slice all the way through the potatoes). Cut one of the potatoes into thin slices, leaving about ¼ inch (6 mm) at the bottom unsliced in order to hold the potato together. Repeat this process with the remaining potatoes and place them, cut side up, in a 12-inch (30-cm) cast-iron skillet.

In a small bowl, mix together all of the ingredients for the herbed butter and spread the herbed butter evenly on the four potatoes sitting in the cast-iron skillet, making sure that you work the butter mixture between the slices.

Place the potatoes in the Big Green Egg and cook them for 55 to 60 minutes, until the potatoes are nicely browned, crisp on the outside and tender on the inside. Garnish them with extra minced parsley and enjoy them as a side dish with your favorite meal.

FEEDS: 8 people

APPROXIMATE COOK TIME:
40 minutes

BIG GREEN EGG SETUP:
Indirect

TOOLS AND ACCESSORIES:
convEGGtor, half-sized
aluminum pan

PIMENTO CHEESE TOPPING

2 tbsp (28 g) butter, melted

1 cup (56 g) panko
breadcrumbs

1 cup (113 g) shredded sharp
Cheddar cheese

8 oz (224 g) cream cheese,
softened

½ cup (120 ml) mayonnaise

¼ tsp garlic powder

¼ tsp onion powder

¼ tsp cayenne

1 (4-oz [112-g]) jar diced
pimentos, drained

MACARONI AND CHEESE

16 oz (454 g) elbow macaroni

1 stick unsalted butter plus 1
tbsp (14 g), divided

2 cups (216 g) shredded
Gruyère cheese

1 cup (113 g) shredded
Cheddar cheese

1 (8-oz [224-g]) block
Velveeta, thinly sliced

2 cups (480 ml) half-and-half

8 slices bacon, cooked and
crumbled

¼ tsp kosher salt

Macaroni and Cheese with Pimento Cheese and Bacon

This recipe combines two of my favorite things: pimento cheese and bacon. Now add that combination to a gooey batch of macaroni and cheese and you have a winning side dish. You can assemble this in advance and cook it in your Big Green Egg when you're ready to serve. You will come back to this recipe time and time again.

Set up the Big Green Egg for indirect grilling (as described on page 20) using the convEGGtor. Preheat the Big Green Egg to 350°F (177°C). While the Big Green Egg is coming up to temperature, prep the pimento cheese topping.

In a small bowl, pour the melted butter over the panko crumbs. Mix the ingredients together well and set the breadcrumbs aside. Make the pimento cheese: Place the Cheddar, cream cheese, mayonnaise, garlic powder, onion powder, cayenne and pimentos in a food processor, and then pulse until everything is well combined. Set the pimento cheese aside while you make and assemble the macaroni and cheese.

Bring a medium pot of salted water to boil over high heat, and cook the macaroni for about 6 minutes, until it is almost done (do not let it become fully tender, as it will get softer when it bakes). Drain the macaroni and return it to the warm pot. Next, add the butter, allowing it to melt as you mix it with the macaroni. Now add the Gruyère cheese, Cheddar cheese and Velveeta to the macaroni. Continue to stir until all the cheeses have been melted and worked in. Slowly add the half-and-half, stirring the mixture constantly to combine the half-and-half with the melted cheeses and macaroni. Finally, add the crumbled bacon, season the macaroni and cheese with the salt and mix everything together thoroughly.

Grease the inside of a half-sized aluminum pan, then pour the macaroni and cheese mixture into it. Spread the pimento cheese mixture across the top, and then sprinkle the panko mixture over that.

When the Big Green Egg has preheated, place the aluminum pan inside and let the macaroni and cheese cook for 30 minutes. When the top is nicely browned and bubbly, remove the macaroni and cheese from the Big Green Egg and let it cool for 5 minutes before serving it.

FEEDS: 4 people

APPROXIMATE COOK TIME:
15 minutes

BIG GREEN EGG SETUP:
Direct

TOOLS AND ACCESSORIES:
Big Green Egg Half Moon
Perforated Cooking Grid

HERBY CHIMICHURRI SAUCE

¼ cup (40 g) finely chopped shallots

½ cup (25 g) finely chopped scallions

2 cloves garlic

1 tbsp (9 g) minced fresh jalapeño

1 cup (16 g) coarsely chopped fresh cilantro

3 tbsp (45 ml) fresh lime juice

¾ cup (180 ml) extra-virgin olive oil

1 tsp kosher salt

1 tsp ground black pepper

ZUCCHINI AND ONIONS

4 zucchini, sliced into ¼" (6-mm)-thick strips

2 white onions, sliced into ¼" (6-mm)-thick rings

1½ tbsp (23 ml) extra-virgin olive oil

1 tsp kosher salt, plus more as needed

½ tsp ground black pepper, plus more as needed

Grilled Zucchini and Onion with Herby Chimichurri Sauce

This is one of two recipes coauthored by my daughter, Jessica (@agranolacoconut on Instagram). When I got to the vegetable portion of the book, I noticed most of my previous work was all meat. I needed inspiration for some vegetable recipes for this section and turned to my daughter, who is an amazing cook and recipe developer. Once I made this for myself, I knew we had a winning recipe for this book. I hope you enjoy making this as much as my family does.

Set up the Big Green Egg for direct grilling (as described on page 18) and preheat it to 400°F (204°C). Place the Big Green Egg Half Moon Perforated Cooking Grid in the Big Green Egg while it is preheating. While the Big Green Egg is coming up to temperature, make the herby chimichurri sauce.

In a blender or food processor, combine all of the ingredients for the herby chimichurri sauce and pulse until all of the ingredients are roughly chopped and evenly combined. Set the sauce aside.

In a large bowl, toss together the zucchini, onions, olive oil, salt and pepper. When the Big Green Egg and grid have preheated, place the zucchini and onions on the grid. Cook them for 2 to 3 minutes, then flip the vegetables and cook them for 2 to 3 minutes on the other side.

When you see a nice char form and the vegetables are tender, remove them from the pan and place them on a cutting board. Chop the vegetables into 1-inch (2.5-cm) pieces. Add some more salt and pepper to taste, then toss the vegetables with the herby chimichurri sauce and serve.

FEEDS: 4 people

APPROXIMATE COOK TIME:
1½–1¾ hours

BIG GREEN EGG SETUP:
Indirect

TOOLS AND ACCESSORIES:
convEGGtor, 12" (30-cm)
cast-iron skillet

1½ cups (360 ml) heavy cream

2 tbsp (28 g) unsalted butter,
melted

4 cloves garlic, minced

2 tsp (1 g) fresh thyme leaves

1 tsp kosher salt

¼ tsp ground black pepper

2½ lb (1.1 kg) russet potatoes

1 tbsp (14 g) butter, softened

1 yellow onion, sliced into
half-moons

2½ cups (270 g) shredded
Gruyère cheese, divided

2 tbsp (6 g) finely chopped
fresh chives

Cheesy Potatoes Au Gratin

Potatoes au gratin was one of my most favorite side dishes my mom would make for us on special occasions. This delicious concoction of potatoes, onion, cream and cheese melts into your soul with every bite. For this recipe, I upgraded the cheese and the milk for a more decadent dining experience. You will thank me after each bite.

Set up the Big Green Egg for indirect grilling (as described on page 20) using the convEGGtor. Preheat the Big Green Egg to 400°F (204°C). While the Big Green Egg is coming up to temperature, prep your cream mixture and potatoes.

Mix together the cream, melted butter, garlic, thyme, salt and pepper in a medium bowl, and set this mixture to the side. Peel your potatoes and slice them ⅛ inch (3 mm) thick using a mandoline or sharp knife.

Coat the inside of a 12-inch (30-cm) cast-iron skillet with the softened butter. Now place a layer of the potatoes on the bottom of the skillet. Layer the sliced onions over the potatoes and then some of the shredded Gruyère cheese. Spoon some of the cream mixture over the first layer and repeat this process until all of the ingredients are used up, reserving ½ cup (54 g) of the Gruyère cheese.

When the Big Green Egg has preheated, cover the pan with aluminum foil and place the pan in the Big Green Egg. Cook the potatoes au gratin for 1 hour and 15 minutes. Remove the aluminum foil and top the potatoes with the remaining cheese. Cook the potatoes au gratin for 15 to 20 minutes, until the cheese has browned and is bubbly.

Carefully remove the cast-iron skillet from the Big Green Egg and garnish the potatoes au gratin with the chives before serving.

APPROXIMATE COOK TIME:
1½ hours

BIG GREEN EGG SETUP:
Indirect

TOOLS AND ACCESSORIES:
convEGGtor, half-sized
aluminum pan

4 russet potatoes

2 tbsp (30 ml) olive oil

½ tsp kosher salt

4 tbsp (56 g) butter, softened

½ tsp celery salt

½ tsp garlic salt

½ tsp ground black pepper

½ tsp paprika

¾ cup (180 ml) sour cream

4 slices bacon, cooked and crumbled

1½ cups (170 g) shredded sharp Cheddar cheese

2 scallions, thinly sliced

Stuffed Baked Potatoes

This is the perfect side dish for your next steak dinner at home. The potato skin is nice and crispy while the filling is creamy and delicious. It may be a good idea for you to double this recipe, as your friends and family will be asking for more.

Set up the Big Green Egg for indirect grilling (as described on page 20) using the convEGGtor. Preheat the Big Green Egg to 375°F (191°C). While the Big Green Egg is coming up to temperature, prep your potatoes.

Wash the potatoes, dry them with a paper towel and then prick the potatoes several times with a fork. Rub the potatoes with the olive oil and season them with the salt.

When the Big Green Egg has preheated, place the potatoes on the grill grate. Shut the lid to the Big Green Egg and cook the potatoes for 45 to 50 minutes, until the potatoes feel soft to the touch and are easily pierced with a fork or temperature probe. Remove the potatoes from the Big Green Egg and let them cool for 15 minutes.

Carefully cut the potatoes in half and scoop the flesh of the potatoes into a medium bowl. Leave a border of flesh that is about ¼ inch (6 mm) thick in the potato skins, which should now look like little boats. Add the softened butter to the potato flesh and mash the potatoes until the ingredients are thoroughly combined. Now stir in the celery salt, garlic salt, pepper, paprika, sour cream, bacon and Cheddar cheese. Mix everything together well and then, using a spoon or piping bag, evenly distribute the filling among the four potato-skin boats you just made.

Place the stuffed potatoes back in the Big Green Egg and cook them for another 20 minutes, until they are nicely browned. Remove the potato skins, garnish them with the sliced scallions and serve them.

FEEDS: 4 people

APPROXIMATE COOK TIME:
15 minutes

BIG GREEN EGG SETUP:
Indirect

TOOLS AND ACCESSORIES:
convEGGtor, 12″ (30-cm)
cast-iron skillet

4 ears corn, kernels removed

½ cup (120 ml) mayonnaise

1 jalapeño, deseeded and diced

1½ tsp (8 g) sugar

4 oz (112 g) shredded mozzarella cheese

2 scallions, thinly sliced

½ tbsp (7 g) softened butter

Kosher salt, to taste

Ground black pepper, to taste

The Buddha's Korean Grilled Corn and Cheese

One item I have been pleasantly surprised to see make the list of banchan (side dish) items at Korean BBQ joints is corn cheese. This tasty dish is an amazing complement to the rich grilled meat served at these restaurants. This is my interpretation of that dish, and it goes great with some of the grilled meat recipes in this book!

Set up your Big Green Egg for indirect grilling (as described on page 20) using the convEGGtor. Preheat the Big Green Egg to 400°F (204°C).

Place the corn kernels, mayonnaise, jalapeño, sugar, mozzarella cheese and scallions in a medium bowl and mix the ingredients together well. Season with salt and pepper to taste. Use the softened butter to grease the inside of a 12″ (30-cm) cast-iron skillet. Pour the corn mixture into the skillet.

When the Big Green Egg has preheated, place the cast-iron skillet inside and let the corn-cheese mixture cook for 10 to 15 minutes. You will know it is done when you see that the mixture has melted and started to bubble. Remove the cast-iron skillet and let the grilled corn and cheese cool slightly before serving it.

Acknowledgments

To my wife, best friend and partner, Debbie Sussman (a.k.a. "Mrs. Buddha")—I couldn't have done this without you. You are and will always be the wind beneath my wings.

To my children, Jessica and Zachary—your presence in my life is the greatest gift. I love and cherish you both.

To my extended Buckman family—John, Judy, Michael, Julie, Madeline and Carter, I am proud to be a member of your family.

Thanks to Snake River Farms for keeping me stocked with the best meat on the market. Dave and McKenzie, you go above and beyond the call of duty. I will always be grateful.

Thank you to Chris Capell and Dizzy Pig BBQ for keeping me stocked with the best rubs and seasonings in the business. Chris, you took me under your wing early on, bringing me to my first EGGtoberfest in 2014 and introducing me to the wider world of competition BBQ. Your mentorship will never be forgotten.

Thank you to John, Rob and Bob at Big Green Egg for giving me the opportunities you have and for your constant support. You trust me to represent your brand, and I work hard daily to live up to that trust.

Thank you to Page Street Publishing. Sarah and Will, you saw the author in me before I saw him in myself. I am eternally grateful for your confidence and support.

Thank you to Gulfport, Florida, a town we are proud to call home. You have accepted Debbie and me into your diverse and creative community. We are forever grateful for the energy and positivity you bring to our lives every day.

Thanks to all of you who follow and support me. I hope I give back a small slice of what I get from you every day.

About the Author

Chris Sussman, a.k.a. The BBQ Buddha, has been a backyard pit master since 2009. He started honing his craft in the Washington, DC, area before making the move to Gulfport, Florida, in 2021. Chris is a founding member of BGE Team Green, which is a sponsored group of the best Big Green Egg social media influencers around the world. Chris and his recipes are regularly featured on the Big Green Egg website and social media channels. During BBQ season you can find Chris cooking at Big Green Egg festivals around the country.

Chris began his BBQ journey in the early 2000s with the purchase of his first smoker. After several years learning how to smoke meat, Chris knew it was time to invest in a new cooker that would meet his needs. After much research, Chris decided the Big Green Egg was the best live-fire cooker on the market and got his first Big Green Egg in 2009. He has been cooking primarily on the Big Green Egg ever since.

In October 2018, Chris decided he was ready to turn The BBQ Buddha into a full-time job. He relaunched the brand and website, expanding his offerings to include catering services and grilling classes. Since that time, Chris's social media presence has exploded, spreading his message of "grilling by feel" to the masses. Between his blog and his YouTube, Instagram and other social media channels, Chris's recipes and techniques have reached millions.

Chris has been featured in major online publications such as *Maxim*, Thrillist and the Huffington Post. Chris has worked with major national brands such as Ace Hardware, Budweiser, Sierra Nevada, Walmart and many others. Chris's first book, *The Four Fundamentals of Smoking*, was published in 2021 by Page Street Publishing.

Index